CW00921490

Cruise a la Carte

*30 Behind-the-Scenes Morsels to Educate
and Delight*

by
Brian David Bruns

A World Waters Publication

Hors d'oeuvres

Something to tantalize and tickle
interest in the crew's life.

Food,
Fun,
Fights,
& More!

What food does the crew eat?

Looking for Grub in All the Wrong Places

Food keeps crew members from fully integrating, perhaps more than any other single thing on the big ships. Access to 'food from home' at sea varies dramatically because 'home' varies dramatically. Some cruise lines have more Indian dishes, or eastern European, or Caribbean, depending on the make-up of the crew. Happily, cruise lines take food for the crew very seriously. It's the real deal—unlike, say, the food court at ye olde shopping mall. Sure, it has Mexican, Italian, and Chinese, but only via Taco Bell, Sbaro's, and Panda, respectively. And those, of course, are hopelessly Americanized. Prior to international corporations, I doubt native Mexicans, Italians, or Chinese would have even recognized such foods as being 'theirs'—especially after eating it. But I digress.

Strangely, ships cater to American tastes below the waterline, despite a dearth of them aboard. The irony is complete when you realize that nearly 100% of said Americans are entertainers who won't eat anything provided. Why? Because hot dogs and hamburgers do not lend themselves to attractive bodies. So why, then, do ships bother? Because hot dogs and hamburgers are cheap. Even better, both can sit under a heat lamp for hours and you'd never know it. Or at least a lad from Indonesia wouldn't. Mystery solved.

But every day on every ship of every cruise line in every sea is Asian day. Copious amounts of steamed white rice are always available for breakfast, lunch, and dinner, bowing to the preponderance of eastern Asian crew. I will never forget my first trip to the crew mess, on *Carnival Fantasy*. While I heaped a couple strip steaks on my plate—myself being nothing if not American—my colleagues opted for a mound of white rice topped by a ladleful of fish head soup. Thus was explained our radical disparity in weight and, perhaps, our temperament.

Fortunately for me, I'm deeply interested in food and found different cuisines from different cultures a benefit. Many did not. Considering how hard we all worked, the desire for familiar, comforting food was understandable. Further, most crew came from rural environments with limited diversity and limited interest in it. Just as a small town lad from, say, Kansas may not be as interested in foie gras as a native of New York City, a small village lad from an island in the Philippines may not be interested in microwave burritos. And after working 80+ hours a week? Let the poor guy have what he wants, for cryin' out loud!

But the real reason foreign crew members hesitate to integrate isn't food: it's food habits.

Food is not allowed in crew cabins, though all crew types sooner or later sneak some in. Many keep a ready supply of dry goods, some of which are occasionally even allowed. Asians, for example, tend to hoard entire flats of instant noodles, and who's going to know about a secreted hot plate, enabling a late night snack? But this maritime discipline restricting food was enacted for a good reason. Two, actually, because on some ships there are roaches.

The real reason food is denied in crew cabins is because it invariably ends up in the toilets in a most nonbiological manner. Ship toilets are very, very sensitive. The crew? Not so much.

When working on Royal Caribbean's *Majesty of the Seas*, we had to contend with this latter issue to the extreme. Fish bones backed up the sewage system so often that the entire aft crew deck smelled like feces. Literally. What killed me was that disposing evidence of illicit nourishment was the only time many flushed the toilets at all! I still shudder at the seeing the overworked zombies brushing their teeth beside toilets filled to the brim, lids wide open. Equally confusing to me was why a crew member flushed a shoe. This resulted in backing up the waste systems for the entire ship, and none other than the hotel director himself was forced to search the cabins for the culprit. There'll be more on that later, but I will add that he swore a lot that day.

Despite all this, some of us aboard do have access to room service. That doesn't mean the crew is happy to provide it, though. One night my order of several sandwiches—I was hosting a party—resulted in bread so deeply impressed by the thumbs of an enraged chef that I could all but see his fingerprints.

What are crew cabins like?

Crew Cabin Surprise

Getting your first roommate in college, for example, can be intimidating, as any life change can be. But getting a new cabin mate on a cruise ship is particularly so. Sharing your limited personal space with a complete stranger is not something common, after all—one-night stands excepted, I guess. But when that stranger is invariably from another nation, indeed probably from another hemisphere entirely, of a different color and different religion speaking a different language, you just don't know what to expect. When approaching my first cabin as crew—when I was a waiter on *Carnival Fantasy*—I thought I was prepared for anything. This was an embarrassing failure of imagination.

B deck cabins were about twenty feet below the waterline. The corridors were taller than on the newer ships, but equally narrow. Poor lighting emphasized the lack of freshness and cast everything in a dismal, back-alley vibe. Thick veins of exposed pipes added to the feeling. None were steaming, but they throbbed. The entire scene could have been a set for the climactic showdown of a bad action movie. My cabin door was horrendously scratched, dented even, as if somehow utilized in a brutal dog-fight. Adding to that impression were the sounds coming through the door: the sharp crack of hand-to-hand combat and cries of pain.

For a crew cabin, the chamber was surprisingly roomy. This

was due to the lack of a sink and a shower to be shared with the neighboring cabin. Such was common on newer ships, but on *Fantasy* such necessaries were down the hall—and horrendously filthy, but that's neither here nor there. Inside were two narrow bunks and two wooden lockers, smudged with age and flaking laminate. A small desk was completely covered by a 13-inch television, the space beneath stuffed with a dorm-sized refrigerator. A single chair hosted a Nintendo. The air was stiflingly hot and stagnant: the vent being hidden behind a securely taped plastic bag that intentionally cut off air flow.

Access to the bunks was blocked by the man who dwelt here: my new roommate. His tiny body lay diagonally across the cabin as to fill it, legs splayed wide open, each foot propped atop its own case of dried noodles. His rear sat deep into a smashed third box, and his head rested on the feet of a huge teddy bear that occupied the lower bunk. The controls of his gaming console sat comfortably on his lap. Though the Nintendo was hooked up to the TV and the controller in his hands, the screen instead blasted a very loud, very obnoxious Asian martial arts movie.

And he was completely naked.

I had never met a man from Thailand before, certainly not one bare-ass naked and spread-eagled in front of me. Such things would become commonplace once I got used to ships, of course.

'Ben', he called himself, because his real name was a whopping eighteen letters long. Upon waking he immediately mentioned his girlfriend was going to sleep with him every night. How two humans and a four-foot teddy bear could share a bunk so small was a marvel. My own head and feet both pressed against the walls, though I, too, had to snuggle with my luggage. But Ben and 'Amy' were quiet and courteous. The only noise they ever made, in fact, was their incessant watching of what appeared to be the same martial arts film over and over and over.

"When are you going to get a new movie?" I finally asked, exasperated.

"It's not the same movie," Ben replied. "It's a forty-part Chinese movie I bought in Malaysia. Dubbed in Korean for Amy. Subtitled in Thai for me."

"On a Japanese TV," I added. "On an Finnish ship under Panama's flag, serving Americans like me."

"See?" Ben exclaimed. "You're learning ships already!"

What are officer cabins like?

Officer Cabin Surprise

Moving up from waiter to manager in Carnival Cruise Lines was literal: the promotion raised me up six decks. No more living below the waterline. Why, if the ship was going down, it would take oodles more time for the water to reach deck four. This was the officer's deck, baby, and I would no longer be subjected to the crew's competing music after the dubiously labelled 'quiet hours' began at 10 p.m. Not that there was ever any question which music—hip hop vs. Bollywood—would win such contests. The latter's strength relied entirely on sheer volume, whereas hip hop's arsenal included volume and bulkhead-vibrating bass and repellant lyrics. But no longer would my four hours of nightly sleep involve my head pressed against a wall literally thumping with bass. No longer would I have to plug my ears over such lyrics as "Yo, yo, I hate cops and bitches, but cops and bitches want me." Alas, the music moved distressingly far towards the other end of the spectrum. Now I listened to "Let your light shine through me, oh Lord, my shepherd."

For my new cabin-mate, a jovial and talkative fellow from northern India, was a Reborn Christian. When Bogo wasn't praying out loud—while showering, shaving, dressing, or really just breathing—he was preaching to the hapless souls within earshot. He had so many Bibles to give away that I had to relinquish my only shelf for the overflow. I would have preferred to gaze at a picture of my girlfriend before falling asleep, but the New Testament was what I got. It was OK, though. Bogo was a good guy. He was probably forty-something, with a graying Persian-style mustache and shaved head. A strange series of indentations marred the back of his skull, not unlike someone pressing their fingers into a wet ball of clay. How he shaved in those grooves I never found out. How he got the horrendous purple circles beneath his eyes I found out all too well.

Oh, did I mention when I first met him he was bare-ass naked? Yeah. In fact, my first three cabins with Carnival all involved strange, foreign, naked men. Ship life.

More trying than the continual reminders that I was going to hell—I failed to repent my sins daily—were the photos of his baby plastered all over the walls. They were horrible, but what could I say? Bogo had been denied leave to see the birth of his son—Carnival Cruise Lines giving no reason—so photos were all the poor guy had. I know he wanted to experience that magical, monumental moment of birth, but honestly, I didn't. Couldn't he have shown photos of a two-minute baby, carefully cleaned and warmly wrapped in a blanket with mom? Instead I was barraged with Junior's first terrifying seconds in this world: discolored, slimy, and screaming. Bogo displayed no less than fifteen blown-up glossy photos by his bunk. They scared me so much I leapt into the top bunk like a child avoiding the monster under his bed.

More trying than even that, however, was that poor, poor Bogo was an insomniac. This I discovered in dramatic fashion.

In the afternoon just two days before, I had left the

charming Transylvanian town where I had vacationed—I carefully omitted any mention of this pagan location to Bogo—and drove four hours to Braşov. At midnight I drove five more hours to Bucharest, followed by a pre-dawn flight to Frankfurt. Then came the eleven hour flight to Chicago surrounded by screaming kids, followed by another five hours flight to New Orleans surrounded by Bourbon Street-bound revelers. Then came the final hour-plus taxi ride to Gulfport, Mississippi.

Though utterly and completely exhausted when I arrived to the ship, I was immediately put to work for no less than fifteen hours straight. I was literally denied even a fifteen minute break. I knew that low-level management always got the worst of it, but ships are insane. My only time off the clock was the ten minutes allocated to leaving the Lido deck, changing my uniform, and getting to the dining room. I worked two dinner seatings and had to physically run to reach the midnight buffet in time.

Thus it was sometime around 3:30 a.m. when I finally got off work and shuffled to my cabin. I had not slept a wink in fifty hours and countless time zones. My eyes burned, my head pounded, and my muscles barely worked. Too tired to even undress, I pulled my heavy body onto the bunk for a glorious six hours of sleep before the next shift. Six! Being an officer was good, after all. Ecstasy was closing my eyes, soothing the itch, watching the redness melt lovingly into cool blackness. I drifted gratefully into slumber... until a voice commanded sharply, "Admit your sins and I will lead you in prayer!"

What is the ship's galley like?

Your Waiter is a Thief

The shortage of necessary materials in a cruise ship dining room is a serious issue, but not for the reason one might think. Each waiter is assigned a specific amount of silverware and a single rack to hold it. Fanatically guarding your silver is a matter of course on Carnival ships, and every rack is profoundly labeled. Because names are extremely confusing on ships— courtesy of 60-some nationalities aboard—many draw pictures instead. As the only American waiter in the fleet, I drew the Stars & Stripes, which may or may not have been more intimidating than my colleague who covered his rack with superbly drawn, realistically creepy bats.

Anyone caught 'borrowing' from a waiter's soiled rack during mealtime faced a severe reprimand. Anyone caught pinching clean silver risked decapitation. At the end of the first seating, waiters would rush their silver to the dishwasher and refuse to leave until the precious cargo was fully cleaned and accounted for. Those who simply hadn't the time for such protection were forced to rely on the goodwill of the dishwashers to keep prying hands away. Needless to say, dishwashers enjoyed a healthy gratuity for ensuring this 'goodwill'. We waiters did not begrudge them, as our less-than minimum wage was generous compared to a dishwasher's salary.

At first, I was disgusted with Carnival's apparent inability to supply their employees with necessary equipment. Every station was required to have X number of saucers, water glasses, wine glasses, silverware, side plates, coffee cups, etc. Yet there was simply never enough of any of these items. Absurdly, a nightly inventory was required and all items were displayed openly upon the tables for counting. Specialty items in particularly high demand were exposed for anyone to steal. Butter dishes were particularly special items, because the guests pinched them, too. So after all that hard work serving guests, waiters endured unpaid guard duty over their stations while waiting for the manager to OK their station. After being cleared and departing, thieving packs of waiters descended upon abandoned stations to gather what they needed for their own inspection. For, to pass the inventory, a waiter was required to steal from another who had already been designated as fully stocked. A nasty consequence of this was that waiters arrived at their stations an hour early—off the clock—to steal it back. Or as much as they could, anyway. The whole thing was bizarre, and completely inimical to the cruise line's insatiable and unrealistic demands for superior service.

And menus? When they were unlocked by a manager the resulting rush would crush less durable employees. The big guys were frequently paid off by the smaller to obtain the precious, understocked menus—paid off or bribed in some manner, which could just as easily include performing laundry services or sex services. While a waiter, I was one of the bigger guys—I'm a corn-fed Midwestern boy, after all—but all deals with my surrounding, pretty waitress neighbors merely involved rolling silverware. Sigh.

Only after observing the restaurant staff did I begin to understand Carnival's policy. The attitude of most waiters was one of extreme indifference towards property. Breakage was exceptionally high because no one cared about the cost. Carnival was a billion-dollar sweat-shop, so why should an over-worked, under-paid waiter care if he dropped a cup? But twenty broken cups a night on each of twenty ships added up in a hurry! By demanding that each station be equipped completely and enforcing it nightly, Carnival threw the responsibility right back onto the waiters. Breakage was thusly low. Frustration thusly high.

Any waiter wanting to get tipped by all his guests—really his only money for the whole cruise—had to focus on preventing breakage. How else can you make happy twenty-six guests simultaneously demanding coffee when you only have ten cups and eight saucers? Despite your best efforts, preparation and/or bribery, pinching-on-the-go was mandatory. Yet even legitimate accidents did not guarantee replacement of necessary equipment. The system was brutal but effective; a metaphor for all things at sea.

What happens on a crew member's first day?

America Means Deodorant

What do you say to a group of thirty scared, exhausted, but excited people who have flown 5,000 to 10,000 miles from home to start a new life at sea? What words can simultaneously console both a macho Bulgarian man and a timid Indonesian woman? The trainer on *Carnival Fantasy's* restaurant college, as it is called, was a small Indian man named Boota. He was kind, gentle, and engagingly handsome. His words, too, were kind and gentle, but below his soothing accent was the hardened steel of experience. Boota did not even address the overwhelming worries that clouded everyone's mind, knowing how they varied so widely. He cut right through concerns—recognizing food, getting lost below decks, doing laundry, contacting home—and made us all focus on what brought us here in the first place.

"Let me welcome you aboard," said the brilliant trainer with a flash of his pretty eyes. "We are going to have a lot of fun, and we are going to do a lot of work. I guarantee this will be a new experience for all of you. It will not be easy. Let's start with why you are here. You're all here for the same reason: money. So to make money, you first need to learn about serving Americans."

I realized what was about to happen. My gut seized in fear. I was going to hear about American behavior and expectations from a third party who had no interest or need to sugar-coat anything. We've all heard of the Ugly American. Was I going to discover that I ranked among them?

"It doesn't matter what things were like back home," Boota continued. "The majority of cruisers are American, so you need to learn what they like and what they don't like. Americans are the easiest people to serve in the world. They're not interested in fine service. They eat out all the time there, so being in the dining room is not a special occasion for them the way it is for most of us. So they don't want a servant: they want a friend. They will ask personal questions about you and your family. They are not being rude, they are trying to make a personal connection. Americans like to talk and these are common conversation starters in their country. Even though it says on your name tag, they'll ask where you're from. They are not being lazy. Again, they are trying to start a conversation. Just don't be upset if they don't know where your country is. Most won't."

Switching gears, Boota began giving more concrete instruction.

"This is an American corporation with American guests, which means American standards. That doesn't mean you must eat hamburgers every day, but it does mean washing with soap and water every day. I'm from India, for example, and lots of Indians smell bad because they don't use soap. That may be fine back home, but it can't happen here. America means deodorant.

"And ships mean English. In guest areas always use English. Even if you are talking about cricket scores in your native language, Americans will assume you're talking about them. Nobody knows why. I guess it's their big sense of personal identity.

"Now let me tell you a true story. A waiter from the Philippines once had a table of old ladies who refused to leave after lunch. He needed them out so he could set up his station for dinner. Finally they ordered more coffee, which was long gone. He had to brew more. It meant he was going to miss preparing for his dinner guests, which probably meant hard time for the second seating, too. He stormed away swearing in Tagalog, using very bad words. He assumed he was safe. But one of the ladies was married to a U.S. military man stationed in the Philippines. She understood every word and told the hotel director. The waiter was forced to apologize and was sent home the very next port, mid-cruise.

"Carnival has over sixty nationalities that get along very well. If we don't, we get sent home. That means no money. If you fight with anybody because he's different, you will be sent home. No money. Even if someone hits you and you don't fight back, you are both going home. Carnival takes it that seriously. Revel in learning about the world, but don't forget why we are here.

"Look around," he said. "These strange foreigners are all here, just like you, for the money. And though it may not seem like it now, by the end of training these strange foreigners will feel like family."

He was right. When the four weeks were up and our group was being dispersed among the fleet, there was not a dry eye in the class.

Do international crews celebrate American holidays?

The Universal Holiday

Religious holidays are not observed on cruise ships because all enforce a policy of 'don't ask, don't tell'. When 60+ nationalities from every corner of the globe cohabit in a very tight space, conversations regarding religion and politics can be troublesome. That said, we're all there for the same reason—money—so such conversations are almost always as they should be: to learn. Your way of life is not threatened because you're far from home. At sea, we're all minorities. Private gatherings are tolerated to observe religious holidays, such as Christmas or Eid or Hanukkah or Holi or you-name-it. The idea of working on cruise ships justifiably leads to the conclusion that you'll learn about other countries in this grand, diverse world of ours. The manner in which such education occurs, however, is not what most preconceive. Crew members rarely get off in ports, and certainly have only a few short, breathless hours to do so. We learn about the world because it's all there below the waterline with us. My best friends on ships represented every religion, race, creed, and economic level.

But what about the fact that most passengers are Americans? For sure, the Fourth of July is a much celebrated day on ships. That is entirely in deference to the passengers who expect such. I've spent many a wild American Independence

Day in Mexico partying harder than even back home. Invariably I was in a tourist-heavy port at the time. When your local business lives or dies by the patrons who frequent it—especially tourists—it behooves one to go with the flow. For the record, my English friends celebrate July Fourth with the same joy as if they, too, were barbecuing in a backyard. Who doesn't like fireworks? Thanksgiving—a personal favorite of mine—is all but ignored on ships, other than the galley straining to prepare copious amounts of turkey. But one American holiday is slowly spreading around the globe. Its origins are shrouded in the misty pagan past, but that is irrelevant to most revelers. What matters is that it's damned fun—pun intended.

Perhaps it's the joy of anonymity behind a mask, perhaps it's a love of ghosts and ghouls, but Halloween is heartily celebrated at sea. Halloween is the one glorious night where you are not only free, but encouraged, to embrace that which brings fear and loathing into the hearts and minds of common man. A cross-dressing man fits into that category as snugly as, say, Freddie Kruger or H.R. Giger's *Alien*. But sometimes you gotta do what you gotta do. My favorite Halloween party on ships was far from the States, in the blue waters of the Mediterranean.

Gathering a Halloween costume of any kind while sailing the Mediterranean is no small task, but was even more so on the *Wind Surf*. Though the world's largest sailing ship, she was still small enough to fit into as many old world ports as you can imagine. Thus we were in port seven days a week, frequently in seven different nations. Cobbling together a unified costume from bits and pieces obtained in Morocco, Spain, France, Monaco, Malta, Tunisia, Italy, Croatia, and Greece is not easy

—especially when none of those countries broadly celebrate the American holiday. Regardless, a Halloween crew party was announced, and nothing brings a shiver down my spine more than the thought of missing a crew party.

But what to be, and how? There were no superstores loaded with costumes, nor seasonal businesses in strip malls. Solutions always present themselves, however, and in my case it was in the form of… well, getting into women's pants. While I admit to constantly thinking about getting into women's pants, that rarely means actually donning them. But this is just what was suggested one evening when brainstorming with a friend from the spa.

"I have nothing to wear," I lamented to Natalie, echoing women everywhere and from all times. Natalie noted this. "You sound just like my cabin mate," she said. "Claudia whined about not having a dress for formal night, so I offered her one of mine." I laughed, while she chortled in her wine. Natalie was six foot two inches tall. Claudia was most definitely not. "You would fit better into one of my dresses," Natalie continued. An idea was born.

So I borrowed a slim black dress from the Australian giantess and next port, Toulon, France, I found a wig shop. It was a real wig shop, that is not silly cheap stuff, but what was I to do? I opted for dirty blonde and shelled out the fifty Euros. Shoes were hopeless for my size twelve and a half feet—we weren't in Vegas, after all—but accessories were encouragingly hurled upon me by the entire spa staff. After great deliberation by the spa girls doing my makeover, I was ordered to shave my goatee. I did. Then came the order to shave my chest. I did not.

Soon enough, however, I was all dolled up and ready for the Halloween party on *Wind Surf*.

When I arrived to the party arm in arm with Natalie, everything came to a screeching halt. Literally: the Italian DJ actually fumbled with his music, horrified. Italian men would rather be hurled into the bowels of hell than be seen without their machismo. The Asian crew stared, agog, while the usually uptight Brits gave me surprisingly 'understanding' nods. Read into that what you will.

Because the *Surf* was so small, the party only involved a few dozen crew members. That doesn't mean we weren't loud enough to wake the dead—some of whom appeared to be joining our booze-swilling ranks. Most costumes were improvised. Natalie wrapped herself toga-like in a white sheet and played Greek goddess. Several spa girls borrowed grease-smeared boiler suits and with the help of lacy bras became... well... slutty engineers. They were very popular, as one could imagine. The Canadian dive instructor grabbed a gondolier outfit in Venice, while the nurse and her husband dressed as the Incredibles. The flamboyantly gay Indonesian photographer just pranced around in his underwear. Oh, he also wore skull makeup. By the end of the party, that was all he still wore. While there was much drinking, it was predominantly an excuse to dance, dance, and dance. As usual, the end of the party saw hook-ups between every race and color. By then I had lost track of how many hands—hairy and otherwise—tried to grope up my dress. Yes, it was quite a party, as crew parties always are.

Do crew members ever fight?

High Seas Cage Match

I began my stint on ships as crew, though I was hired to be management. I am grateful for my time as a crew member, a cog in the wheel. Not surprisingly, becoming management did nothing to change my status as a cog in the wheel… and I am less grateful for my getting quickly demoted back to crew. After my first year or so at sea, I switched to something else entirely: I became an art auctioneer. This placed me between both worlds, as a staff member—not to be confused with a crew member—living in guest areas, yet also management of crew members. It was a position fraught with tension from all sides.

One would think that having my own, personal guest cabin would at least protect me from unwelcome surprises due to strangers. No naked men upon first entering my room, for example. One would be wrong. First sight of my cabin on *Sensation* was a doozy. It was an interior guest cabin with beds against two different walls. The room reeked of fish.

"What's with the separate bunks?" I asked my departing counterpart, an Australian auctioneer named Robin. "Aren't you here with your girlfriend?"

He was about to answer when a very tall, attractive woman entered. She was six feet tall and, while pleasantly slender, still built solid. Her long hair was naturally blonde, but the last six inches were dyed black. She wore a cowboy hat and boots over snug blue jeans. Vanessa was her name. The cowgirl answered the question on behalf of Robin, "He stinks. He belches all night, so I want as much distance as possible."

"You like cod liver oil?" she suddenly asked, whirling to face me.

I was prompted to reply, rather cheekily, "Are you asking me on a date?"

She gestured broadly to the room. "We've got plenty for ya. I'm sick of 'em. If I smell one more damned pill, I'm gonna puke. Loverboy here don't eat no food, jus' lives off cod liver oil."

A quick glance proved Vanessa wasn't joking. I counted no less than four bottles of cod liver pills of varying sizes. A fifth bottle lay on its side on a bunk behind where Robin sat, looking suspiciously as if it had dumped its contents between the cushions. A family sized jar with a wide mouth was currently open, the smell of heavy fish oil almost visually emanated from it.

"Aren't you supposed to refrigerate those once opened?" I asked in wonder.

Robin scoffed, "Bah! You Yanks always worry about stuff like that."

"So'd you tell him yet?" Vanessa asked Robin.

He ignored her, but she pressed the question. Robin reacted strongly, and suddenly both were glaring at each other, postures frozen in defiance: she tall and leaning willowy-strong over him, he looking up to meet her with bulldog neck tensed and fists clenched. He finally spat, "Shut up, woman!"

Offended, Vanessa snatched up the nearest bottle of fish oil pills—the family sized jar sans lid—and hurled it at him.

Delicate globules of smelly fish oil sprayed wide, bouncing off Robin to clatter off the walls, the desk, the bed and everything else until they found every last corner.

Robin snarled, reaching for her. She gamely bounced back, but this was no game. They exchanged all manner of insults, voices rising until she screeched and he bellowed. Finally he muscled his way in to give her a solid slap across the face. The sound was shockingly loud. Violence in person is completely unlike anything in the movies. It was immediate, intimate, horrible.

"Oh!" she cried in surprise, hair flinging wild.

I leapt in between the two of them, now shouting myself. I had no idea what was going on, even as I sensed this was not an unusual occurrence between them. Indeed, before I could interfere they both whirled upon me as one.

"This is none of your business, Yank!" Robin bellowed.

"I can handle this myself!" Vanessa echoed. She was already returning her attention to her adversary, adding, "I'm from Texas!"

Vanessa delivered a tremendous blow of her own, a wallop that sent Robin reeling. Before he had a chance to recover, she shoved him onto the bed. Next came a sharp crack of head hitting bulkhead, and Robin collapsed. He gave a low moan, and Vanessa was atop him. Then they began madly kissing, passionately rolling across the tiny bunk... and grinding cod liver pills into my future mattress.

I never again saw Robin and Vanessa together, but I smelled them every night.

What does the crew do for fun?

Gold Medal for Outstanding Performance!

Olympic gold medalist Hope Solo has vindicated what I've been saying since I wrote *Cruise Confidential*.

"There's a lot of sex going on," she stated to ESPN in July, 2012. "With a once-in-a-lifetime experience, you want to build memories, whether it's sexual, partying, or on the field. I've seen people having sex right out in the open. On the grass, between buildings, people are getting down and dirty."

She was talking about the Olympic Village, but if you inserted 'crew cabins' she would have been right on the money. Swimmer Ryan Lochte—another multiple gold medalist— backed Solo up, stating he believes "70 percent to 75 percent of Olympians" hook up behind the scenes. He added slyly, "Hey, sometimes you gotta do what you gotta do."

But these are Olympians, humans who do stuff daily the rest of us would find impossible, right? Enter your cruise ship waiters. They work every day, all day, for up to ten or more months straight. Sure, the time-clocks say only 80 hours a week, but we all know that doesn't include time spent guarding your station from roving packs of waiters, hungry for your saucers and side plates. Many of us showed up an hour early before every shift, and nearly every day that means three shifts. All that's on top of boat drill: both passenger's and crew's. Yet crew still find plenty of time to hook up, and not necessarily in their cabins, either. I've seen crew going at it on open decks. A particularly wild crew party on *Carnival Fantasy* comes to mind —as narrated in *Cruise Confidential*.

At sea the reasons for this wild abandon are very much the same as in Olympic Village. Despite coming from every corner of the globe, everybody is there for the same reason. They're all far from home, working hard at something nobody back home can possibly relate to. All are generally young, generally attractive, and generally can't get on board unless proven squeaky clean. Many are looking to make memories, many are desperate to feel good for just a few minutes. Finally, many have never experienced freedom from parental—or village— scrutiny before. Anonymity after growing up with three generations in a three room home in a small town? Think about it.

Oh, and ships provide free condoms.

More than 100,000 condoms were distributed to athletes for the London Olympics, according to Yahoo contributor David C. Cutler. It took only one week for athletes at the Olympic Village at the 2000 Sydney Olympic Games to run out of the 70,000 condoms supplied. See? Similarities between Olympians and crew are rising. Funny how cruise lines won't reveal just how many condoms they distribute. Those of us who lived below the waterline certainly know.

Working on a cruise ship is a work-hard, play-hard lifestyle. For most of us, it's only for a short period in our lives, when we're young and adventurous. Why not make the most of it? You have a world-wide smorgasbord of bodies to choose from, probably for the only time in your life. That's worth losing a little sleep over. And for those who still don't believe that crew can party like Olympians and still function in the morning, I offer Hope's parting words to ESPN:

"When we were done partying, we got out of our nice dresses, got back into our stadium coats and, at 7 a.m. with no sleep, went on *The Today Show* drunk."

Abandoned diary of a cruise ship worker

I stumbled onto this blog by 'Crewbar Queen,' begun on two separate sites several years ago. She obviously held a staff position, based on the ease of her entry into ships. She didn't see it that way. Her words, filled with anxiety and confusion, moved me. All crew can relate to her every word. Below is her only post:

"It's Sunday and I joined the ship today. I am already exhausted. I look around as I type this, staring at the four walls of this closet size cabin with four beds in it. Soon my roommates will be off work so I am glad I was able to shower before they get back. One bathroom, four beds, one TV, one other Canadian, a Filipino Girl and a Romanian. I can't remember their names yet. The Romanian girl seemed stuck up as hell. In fact, so did most of the Romanian girls I met today.

"I wonder what I am doing here. From the second I stepped on board today, I have been pulled in every direction, fitted for an ugly red uniform, thrown into a boring three hour safety class which pretty much has me fearing a *Titanic*-like experience now, and I have been lost three times.

"I am starting work tomorrow. I will just stand alongside some girl who seems to struggle with the English language, and learn as I go. 2000 guests got off the ship today and another 2000 got on. I am feeling a little overwhelmed at the amount of knowledge I need to have. Everyone here seems so intense. The Safety Manager flipped out on me and this other Canadian girl

when we were late for class today. He actually threatened to
send us back home before we left port. I never realized I would
need to know how many lifeboats a ship carries, or how to
evacuate the passengers. Isn't there a captain and some sort of
safety squad for that??

"I kind of miss home. I packed my life into cardboard boxes
in less than a week and left every comfort zone I was sheltered
by. The small voice inside of me that I normally ignore finally
spoke loud enough to get me here, and now it's still trying to
talk me through it. This is supposed to be a chance to see the
world and an opportunity to grow.

"Later - My roommates are back and I am sitting in bed.
The Romanian girl's name is Alina. She hardly said two words
to me when she got here, but she sure is full of conversation for
this guy in her bed now. All I can hear is her giggling and his
deep Caribbean accent. I guess he's her boyfriend. I didn't
realize we could fit another body into this cabin. Wait...is she
really....what the f@#$, they are screwing!

"Does she not realize two other people are in this room?
Does she seriously think this curtain that closes around each
bunk is sound proof?? I open my curtain and look across at the
bunk next to me where the Filipino girl, Carmella, is sitting. I
look at her as if to say, "is this really happening?". She smiles
obliviously and keeps staring at the TV, slurping her instant
noodles. Clearly, this is something she is used to. I'm logging
off for the night. I'm not to used to falling asleep to live porn, I
think I'll pop in some of these ear plugs they gave us to drown
out the sound of the engine and try to get some sleep."

Entrées

*Items savory and serious, satisfying
hunger for maritime knowledge.*

*Sinking,
Survival,
Sickness,
& Other Such Fun*

The Truth About Falling Overboard

Like in any big city, on a cruise ship few stars can be seen at night. Even if sailing black waters with black sky far from mankind, the ships themselves blast so much light pollution that you can see nothing but black. It's precisely how and why stars are not visible from the surface of the moon.

I pondered this one night while at the stern rail. Aft, port, and starboard were all inky, impenetrable black. Far beyond the bow, I knew, the orange glow of oil refineries illuminated moments in the swamps of Louisiana. For we were nearing the mouth of the Mississippi River, the proximity of which was occasioned by navigational beacons of red and green popping through the broken surface of the sea.

"What happens if I fall overboard?" a man had asked me earlier.

It was such a common question that my answer had become habit. "The ship will stop and a boat will pick you up."

Such was the truth, if only half of it. I gazed into the wake of the ship and watched the brown water churn. The waves looked very small indeed from the top decks. If the hundred-plus foot fall did not kill the passenger, he would utterly disappear in the giant swells. Fortunately, it is unlikely modern azipod propellers would chop him into chum, because the propellers remain safely below the hull, rather than behind it. I almost wonder if such a fate would be better, though. Certainly quicker and less terrifying than being alone in the dark, desperately struggling to remain atop that delicate skin of surface above the gargantuan, unfathomable volume of unknown below you. Then you tire, sink, and become one with it.

Safety training was very clear in the case of a man overboard: first throw a life-ring, then call the bridge. People assume the life-ring is simply a flotation device, but it is in fact much more. A person's head will disappear from sight within seconds from the deck of a big ship. After throwing a life ring we were trained to grab someone, anyone, to physically point at the swimmer and not stop until he's found, no matter how long it takes. That physical act of pointing is paramount, for even if aware of the swimmer, he'll be lost in less than one minute at sea. But at night? And if no one sees you fall?

Goodbye.

That very cruise someone had, in fact, gone overboard. Rumors of how and why among passengers and crew were rampant. The leading story among the former being that two honeymooners were arguing and there was a push. Crew thought differently. Another suicide, most agreed. For suicides are not so rare on cruise ships. More than a few folks intentionally spend their every last penny on a final week of wild abandon and, late on the final night, jump overboard. What better way to ensure no one will rescue you? How many people are looking aft of a ship at 3 a.m.? It is possible to survive such falls, but unlikely unless you're a fighter.

Though statistically utterly insignificant, unexplained deaths on cruise ships do happen. Because most occur in international waters, reporting obligations and behavior are decidedly less than altruistic. Cruise lines invariably fudge reporting, because people read headlines, not articles. Whether it's a suicide or not matters little to critics, who pounce upon any hint of cruise line recklessness. Even if it is a suicide, days can pass before verification from land-based authorities, even with the presence of a note. By then, sensational headlines would have already blown things wildly out of proportion.

But any premature death is a tragedy. This much is true. All should be investigated and ships aren't transparent enough. That is also true. But do we need to be worried about dying on a ship? That's the question to ask. According to David Peikin of CLIA (Cruise Lines International Association), between 2003 and 2012 there were 59 fatalities resulting from ships' operations. That's out of 239 million passengers who sailed, and not including natural causes or falling overboard.

59 out of 239,000,000.

Hmm….

Between 2003 and 2008, 108 people died from cattle-induced injuries across the United States, according to the CDC (Centers for Disease Control and Prevention). America's population is a tad higher than the statistic quoted—240M vs. 300M or so—but that still makes cows twice as likely to kill you than anything on a cruise ship. Further, that cow statistic is for only a five year period, whereas the cruise article is citing eight years. Even more surprising is that driving accidentally into a cow on the road is not part of this statistic. Thus, pure cow malevolence is twice as likely to kill you as being on a cruise. Am I being flippant? Of course. But humor is a great way to dispel fear, especially irrational fear.

On that dark cruise outside the swamps of Louisiana,

nobody knew for certain what happened, what caused the mysterious death. An investigation was eventually resolved somewhere on land, as was always the case. The only fact the crew knew for sure was that the man was never found until he washed up on the Gulf Coast several days later.

I focused on a floating piece of flotsam and watched it disappear into the night. I counted off the moment. It was lost to the blackness within fifteen seconds.

Are Cruise Ship Doctors Safe?

Few things bring out fear, prejudice, and ethnocentrism more completely than medical care on cruise ships. We're all subject to a bit of this. After all, when ill, who doesn't prefer mom's chicken soup over an injection, regardless of how credentialed the medical professional may be? Alas, mom's not on the cruise, so we have to rely on the ship's medical staff.

But is he/she credentialed? Yes.

Is he/she what you are used to at home? No.

Does it matter? Probably not.

First, the scare tactics: an oft-cited paper by Consumer Affairs in 2002 found medical facilities on ships lacking. They were quite harsh without actually providing much data. For example, they claimed a survey conducted by the American Medical Association found 27% of ship doctors and nurses did not have 'advanced training' in treating heart attacks. They did not define 'advanced training,' so even a gastroenterologist serving a stint at sea could easily be considered unqualified. Yet these 'severely lacking' individuals, as the article literally labelled them, have a success rate that puts U.S. hospitals to shame. Indeed, losing merely .000004% of such patients are odds I'll take any day! Those are numbers cited in that very same article. The language was damning. The numbers were not.

Cruise ship doctors rarely see passengers for anything beyond dehydration or tummy ache. The overwhelming majority of medical issues you'll have on a cruise will be what you brought with you: heart attacks being most common. Time is the most important issue in treating heart attack, not size of the facility.

Still not convinced? Consider: "living on a cruise ship provides a better quality of life and is cost effective for elderly people who need help to live independently", says a study published in the Journal of the American Geriatrics Society (2004). Many elderly, high-risk folks hop from ship to ship to ship, more than satisfied with ship facilities and personnel.

A brilliant article from CNN Health explains much of ship doctor training: http://brev.is/pzt3

I've met many a cruise ship nurse and doctor. More than a few are American surgeons and nurse practitioners who have taken tours as ship medical personnel for a change of pace. But most ship doctors are not licensed in the U.S. That doesn't mean they haven't been licensed professionals for a great many years back home. That home may be from Europe, for example, or Africa. This is where ethnocentrism rears its ugly head. Whispers of witch doctors. I've read online complaints— usually from my fellow Americans—of "some African doctor identifying my wife's ailment as caused by her sins and prescribing a bath in the blood of Jesus Christ." I find this as plausible as reports of Elvis sightings.

Ultimately, cruise lines are not required to provide medical care at all. You are placing yourself under the perceived protection of a corporation; corporations that intentionally pay taxes in one country, register ships in another, hire employees from many, take passengers from yet more, then sail where there are no laws at all. If you have an underlying medical condition or concern, it behooves you to take responsibility for your own care by research and preparation. As ships often mention, their medical facilities are the equivalent of a small town. If a medical emergency occurs that is beyond the abilities of the ship, you will be helicoptered off to the nearest hospital. If that's not in the U.S., so be it. If you are that terrified of the rest of the world's standards, then don't leave home.

Why Galley Tours Are Useless

*Warning: profanity implied within—only implied, but we're talkin' about sailors here!

New York Stock Exchange on a Sunday night.

Bourbon Street on a Monday morning.

Cruise ship kitchen on a galley tour.

All are silent, empty sights unable to convey the absolute bedlam and pandemonium perpetrated there daily. The echoes have died, the detritus of maelstrom removed: ticker tape swept, bottles recycled, grills scraped.

I understand the desire to join a galley tour. I, too, am a foodie and interested in the functioning of the facility. But a galley tour does nothing, absolutely nothing, to convey the reality of a cruise ship galley under fire. For cruise ship galleys are not about equipment, nor layout, nor routine. They are not about the useless statistics guides boast of—zillions of dishes served in mere minutes, and the like. Cruise ship galleys are about the workers sweating and swearing and stealing within.

Swearing and stealing? That never happened at the chef's table inside the kitchen, you say. Yeah, and I'm sure your teenage kids behave exactly the same after you leave them alone at the house for the weekend.

Galley tours are organized groups pulsing through shiny stainless steel corridors like blood pumping through a healthy heart; meal times are a violent cardiac arrest, with bodies straining against blockage. As time ticks by the heart palpitates

and everyone and everything pushes harder, louder, more
erratically. But bodies pooling by the front line have nowhere to
go. Pressure rises and things turn ugly. Eventually, at every
meal something will rupture and waiters must scamper and run
every which way, like internal bleeding.

Too graphic a metaphor, you think? Hardly. It's a jungle in
there. Cruise ship waiters squabble over hash browns like
hyenas fighting for scraps stolen from a lion's kill. It's survival
of the fittest, and it's all for you, dear cruiser.

I will never, ever forget the first time I was assigned to pick
up the hot food at breakfast in the dining room on *Carnival
Conquest*. I had been given sixteen orders simultaneously. So
had everyone else. Simultaneously.

"Hi, chef," I began, reading aloud my order to the frenetic
Indian chef with black skin, "I need, uh, six orders of eggs over-
easy, two with pancakes, one with bacon, one with pancakes
and bacon, two with sausage and bacon, and one with pancakes,
sausage, bacon, and hash browns. I need two orders of eggs
over-hard with pancakes and sausage, and..."

"New boy, out of my way," interrupted another waiter. He
elbowed me aside and bellowed, "SIX OVER-HARD,
PANCAKES, BACON, BROWNS! Let's go!"

"Hey, Filipino," an Indian waiter chided. "Leave the guy
alone. Chef, ignore him and the American. Help a fellow
Indian. Give me four scrambled, two with browns, four
with...."

"Rasclat," someone shouted, "Get your hands off my
pancakes!"

"Hey!" everyone cried as a Bulgarian butt in.

"Those are my hash browns, you bastard! I need four scrambled, two with bacon, one with sausage, and one with browns. Get on it, chef!"

"F@*# you! Chef, are those my hash browns?"

"Kiss my ass, Euro-boy," the chef finally retorted. "Colonize someone else!"

"Hey, why are you giving him my eggs?" I whined. "America never colonized anybody."

"You bomb everybody," snapped someone in the bristling crowd of waiter. "Take my oil but not my eggs!"

"What blood clot took my over-easies? Chef, lay those eggs faster!"

"Do I look like a chicken to you?" the chef retorted. "You know any black chickens, motherf@*#er?"

"Get your f@*#ing jelly off my tray, a$#hole!"

"How you say chicken in your white-monkey language?" needled a second Indian chef, backing up his colleague.

"F@*# you!"

"No, f@*# you!"

"F@*# you both. Were are my sausages? Not the f@*#ing links, the f@*#ing patties, blood clot!"

At that point everyone dropped civility and the language turned truly ugly.

The kicker? Breakfast in the dining room involved only about 10% of the waiters aboard. Enjoy the tour, 'cause you sure as hell don't wanna be in there during a real dinner!

The Truth About Art Auctions

There is much to enjoy in an art auction aboard a cruise ship. The auction process can be quite entertaining for those who participate, and art itself can bring stimulation into even the most dreary life. Yet there is much to fear. I have been a professional artist, art historian, and art dealer, and can assure you that being fleeced by an art dealer is by no means restricted to ships. First I will discuss some tips about the art world in general, then specifically about art sales on cruise ships.

The easiest way to catch a lying salesperson, be it in gallery or auction, is when talking about limited editions. Watch for lines like 'the lower the number, the more valuable the work', or 'the first numbers are crisper because the plates are fresher' or 'artist's proofs are worth more.' These are common lies art dealers tell to increase the price.

First of all, every work of a limited edition from any reputable atelier (workshop) is certified before it leaves, and if it's not as perfect as all the others then no reputable artist would sign it.

Second, and far more revealing, is how the process works: hand-made lithographs—made on metal plates nowadays but traditionally on a stone—have a different plate for each color and use semi-transparent inks for blending. Hand-made serigraphs, in the same manner, use a different screen. That's a lot of plates, which means a lot of human error. So to get an edition of 100, you start with 200 runs of the first color plate, then throw out the mistakes (smudging, etc.). Now you have

193 left, for example, and run on top of those the second color plate. Throw out the mistakes that don't align right, etc. and move on down the line of color plates until done. By the end you'll have your 100, and probably a few left over.

Those remaining works—identical to the 100 in every way —are labeled AP (artist proof) or PP (printer's proof) or whatever else they care to call it.

Thomas Kinkade, for example, made up dozens of such tags to give the illusion of exclusivity. The irony in his case was that much of his artwork wasn't produced by hand and was in all ways merely a poster.

The point is that there is no 'first print pulled' or 'artist color check' or any of that crap. All were assembled simultaneously. It's physically impossible to do otherwise. Thus, limited editions all have an identical tangible value. Until they begin to sell out, of course. Art is very much about supply and demand.

Ultimately, the real value of art is simply what someone wants to pay for it. That's why Picasso paintings sell for $100M. He's the most famous artist in history and he's not making any more paintings. Simple as that.

Beware the sales tool pushing art as an investment. That's pure gambling. The biggest gains are always from the biggest risks. Is that a game you really want to play? How many people really wanted to shell out tens of thousands of dollars for a Jackson Pollock splatter painting back when the average house cost $14,500? As luck—and a surprise encounter with a horny, eccentric zillionaire art buyer and a dramatic, early demise— would have it, such a painting would now be worth millions.

Yet most who bought Pollock's works did so because they enjoyed his art for one reason or another, and that's the only reason to buy art. Because you like it.

Buying art is like buying a car. The more you know about it, the less you can be had by a salesman. In Venice I went to an art dealer in Piazza San Marco selling Picassos. They were limited editions complete with certificates of authenticity for a few thousand euros, which I knew was about $1/80^{th}$ the going price for what I was looking at. After scrutinizing the work a moment, I realized they were limited edition machine lithographs of an original Picasso limited edition hand-press etching. In other words, they Xeroxed the expensive Picasso and sold the copies in small batches. The certificate of authenticity was from the local company churning out the Xeroxes.

So what about art auctions at sea? I have a lot to say about art auctioneers, dishing on them—us—heavily in my book *Ship for Brains*.

Because of international waters, are they inherently less trustworthy than galleries on land? No. Losing a contract with the cruise line is a killing blow for a gallery, so they won't blatantly scam people—at least they didn't in my day. But that doesn't mean individual art auctioneers weren't liars. Many were in my days and I doubt it's changed much.

One auctioneer, for example, promised a private lunch with the world-famous artist Peter Max with every purchase of a limited edition. Ludicrous he said it. Ludicrous people bought it. Eventually word of such antics forced the art gallery to videotape every auction and scrutinize every auctioneer for lies. Labor intensive, to be sure, but credibility is everything in the art world.

The most common question from American buyers was always: why is it so expensive? If you can't tell the difference in quality between a $15 poster and a $1500 lithograph from Marcel Mouly, or are disdainful of any such difference, then collecting art isn't for you. Some may take offense at such a statement, but collecting art simply isn't for everyone. Art auctions sell quality art. Well, there's some crap, too: they are selling to the general public, after all, which means high end and low. But art auctions provide an opportunity to learn the difference between that Star Wars poster still on your wall and a lithograph from a French atelier that worked with Picasso. It's OK to have both. I do.

And, just for the record, in college I learned to create lithographs, serigraphs, copper-plate etchings, and linoleum cuts to earn my degree as art historian. It's freakin' hard.

The most common misconception from American buyers was always: how can it be original if there is more than one? This concept is unique to us from the States. Maybe it comes from our inherent need for individuality, I don't know. I do know it's wrong. The vast majority of Americans are not educated about art: didn't take classes in school (high school or college), don't have it at home (or know anyone who does), don't go to art museums, and don't spend time discussing its relevance (modern or historical). We are an extremely art-illiterate society. That's OK. Yet those very same people insist that to be an original work means there is only one, such as a painting. That's not OK. Admitting ignorance is the first step to overcoming it.

Anything that is made by hand by an artist is an original work of art. It's a craft.

Art auctions on ships provide an introduction into a vastly complicated world. Can you learn all there is to know about wine—domestic, import, vintages, varietals, not to mention taste, bouquet, procedures, etal.—in a short presentation? Or when buying a car? Understand that auctions cater to the masses of unsophisticated buyers. It's their business, it's your opportunity. If you are serious about collecting art, do your homework. Are your best interests in mind when you're educated by a salesman? I think not. If you're worried about a good price, buy it outside the auction so you can haggle down instead of bidding up. Why, oh why do people forget that the whole darn point of an auction is to get the prices higher?

If you are there for the excitement of an auction, great! Have fun. It's not rigged, you're just in their house and playing into their strengths, not yours. Auctions get people excited and they act impulsively. Most complainers aren't scammed: they're embarrassed. And, really, when any salesman gives you free booze, be careful!

Corruption of Cruise Ship Security

Is cruise ship security corrupt? So many things about the industry are, why not the guards? Do they let drugs aboard in the luggage of passengers, of crew? Do they turn a blind eye to certain illegal activities which are, of course, not illegal in international waters? I have indeed seen cruise ship security being paid off...

2 a.m.

I nervously enter the crew cabin way down on B Deck. Victorio, a serious-looking Filipino, motions me to sit. Both bunks already hold two or three men, all of whom dropped their conversation at the sight of me. The bathroom door lay open to reveal several more men, also regarding me. They are surprised to see me, but say nothing. The floor of both tiny chambers is fully occupied by coolers, which I have to somehow tiptoe over. Unsure of myself, I wiggle in beside the others. I do not belong here.

Victorio asks, "You bring it?"

A flash of nerves jolts me. Shaking my head, I defend, "I just found out an hour ago. I'll bring it tomorrow."

Victorio regards me solemnly for a moment. The cabin remains silent, but for the surge of waves outside the bulkhead.

"If you didn't bring it," Victorio asks, "Why you come here?"

I glance around, noting all the eyes staring at me, waiting.

Slowly Victorio stands. He is large for a Filipino man, but

still smaller than my corn fed American self. He approaches, saying softly, "We do things different than you Americans...."

I cringe as he towers over me. He holds something behind his back, I don't know what. His cohorts press me from the sides. What was I thinking, coming here so late, with nothing to offer?

Suddenly Victorio grins.

"In the Philippines, birthday means we buy the drinks, not get gifts."

His hands move, revealing what he'd been holding. A plastic cup filled with scotch.

"So have a drink," Victorio orders. Then, to get the party in full swing, he bellows, "We have an American, boys!"

Cheers come for diversity. Drinks come to my hand. Nearby bristles two bottles of Johnny Walker Blue Label scotch, two Black Labels, three bottles of Chivas Regal, and two coolers icing Coronas. Victorio predicts that by 5 a.m. all will be empty. We feast on traditional Filipino foods—or close as could be made aboard. My favorite are strips of cold beef marinated in lime juice and exotic seasonings. I sense they are pleased I enjoy a taste unique to their homeland.

By 3:30 a.m. the party is really rocking—as much as possible with no women present, anyway—when someone brings out a small, black torture device. Terror seizes my soul. It is a karaoke machine, complete with microphone and two large speakers—so large, in fact, Victorio has to sleep with one in his bunk. Cheers resound in eardrum-crumpling waves.

"You can't turn that on," I protest. "It's 3:30 a.m.!"

"We got it covered," Victorio assures me.

For some sinister reason, karaoke is a great joy for Filipinos, with a particular passion for rock ballads. Invoking Bon Jovi prompts hands over hearts. One waiter, Jeffry, is so talented that he entertains guests in the dining room. His crystalline voice cuts through the chatter every time. His cover of Michael Bolton is barely distinguishable from the real thing. And Jon Secada? They must surely be twins. But this night Jeffry does not want to sing. He wants me to sing. I demur. They press.

"Who wants to hear Brian sing Elvis?" Jeffry cries.

The cabin reverberates with a roar of approval.

Spontaneity—or more likely, alcohol—encourages me. I finish off my scotch and say, "Filipino party: Filipino music. Bring it."

"I thought you liked singing Elvis," he said.

"Oh, I'll sing it like Elvis all right."

The television features a surging tropical beach while Filipino lyrics pass by staggeringly fast. Certainly too fast for one who can't read Tagalog. I had hoped their native language didn't use Roman characters so I could wiggle out of it. No such luck. Soon my best Elvis voice sings a sappy love ballad to twenty drunken Filipino men—and the entire B Deck of *Carnival Conquest*.

"Tinapon ng lalaki ang bola sa pader... something... something fried banana sandwich... thank ya, thank ya vury much.... Say, what did I just say?"

"You just tried to say 'the boy threw the ball at the wall'."

"How romantic. A hunk'a-hunk'a burnin' love I'm not."

A pounding at the door. Silence falls. Victorio reluctantly

opens the doors, revealing an insanely muscled security officer. Two more men flank this largest Asian man ever. He frowns angrily, flexes his muscles.

"You're in BIG trouble," he booms. "You paid me to leave you alone... on the condition I sing, too! I don't get off until four!"

Ye Plague Facts

You need to know two things to understand the norovirus issue that plagues us every year—pardon the pun. Surprisingly, neither covers how to avoid getting it, though the second point is absolutely the single most important overlooked fact in understanding the issue.

First: norovirus is not just a ship problem.

In fact, it's barely on ships at all, compared to how many land-based institutions are struck every year right in your own city. Norovirus is common throughout all of North America and Europe, being most prevalent in schools, hospitals, nursing homes, and children's day care facilities. It strikes every year.

Norovirus on land is so regular, in fact, it no longer incites headlines. Those are now reserved for the unusual, the exotic, such as "PLAGUE SHIP!" An illness transmitted from your children isn't nearly as alarming as "RATS SPREAD DISEASE!". But you get a cold or flu from your kids all the time. That headline wouldn't sell many newspapers.

Yet the land numbers are far, far greater than the sea numbers.

There were 2,630 confirmed reports of norovirus in autumn 2012 in the United Kingdom, for example. Yet for every reported case there are likely to be a further 288 unreported sufferers, according to the Health Protection Agency (HPA). Recent figures from the HPA show that more than 750,000 people could be affected by the 2012 outbreak of norovirus in the U.K. alone. It's so bad, in fact, that they're closing hospital wards and denying visitors access to the buildings. Take Birmingham City Hospital, for instance, which closed three wards due to norovirus infection, or Doncaster and Bassetlaw Hospitals, which actually tweeted, "Please don't visit hospital until at least two days after last symptoms of vomiting or diarrhea. Stay home, rest, and take fluids."

But nobody thinks about infected hospitals down the street. They think of cruise ships. They think of sensational headlines. Take the media frenzy surrounding the P&O liner *Oriana*, dubbed 'a plague ship.'

"It's a living nightmare."

"Scores of passengers laid low by virus."

"People were falling like flies, yet the crew were trying to insist everything was fine."

Oh, the drama!

The sick have vomiting and diarrhea a few days, tops, and possibly stomach cramps. If that's your definition of 'a living nightmare', you suffer from a serious lack of real life. You'll note the hospital referred to above even told sufferers to stay home and chill out. Subjective perceptions of severity aside—I know it sucks, but you're not dying or victim of any cruise line skullduggery—let's look at real numbers. More importantly, what's behind them. It's not what you think at all.

An outbreak, according to the U.S. Center for Disease Control, is 3% or higher of reported passengers and crew being sick. Please note the inclusion of 'crew'. When one crew member is sick, all of his/her cabin mates—whether sick or not —are automatically quarantined and counted as sick. Thus, the number of infected crew is artificially inflated by double or more from the very beginning.

But the inflation of numbers snowballs immediately. Remaining crew members shoulder the additional workload— with no increase in pay, of course. Indeed, if a crew member is out sick for only a couple of days, their tips are not redistributed to the hapless individuals who had to pick up the slack on top of their already overwhelming work load. For, as a rule all crew members are already overworked and nearly all live in a state of near-exhaustion. It is not surprising, then, that many crew members jump on the bandwagon and call in sick just to get a paid, glorious eight hours of sleep—something which they probably haven't had in ten months.

Thus comes the second, and most important, aspect of the plague ship phenomenon. An official outbreak of norovirus on a cruise ship could very realistically involve only 1% of the people aboard. In fact, it's more than likely; it's almost assured. I don't know about you, but I don't think 1% of the population being sick during cold and flu season to be the definition of 'a living nightmare.'

When Ships Collide

Working midnight buffet, I sensed something was wrong. Ketchup bottles slid to port. All of them, in unison. Any sharp turn was amplified up here on deck 14, sure, but *Conquest* kept listing further... further....

Silverware bundles tumbled off tables. Then plates. The ship keeled more. Waiters were ordered to the dish room to manually hold up stacks of plates and saucers. Glasses were deemed safe in their washing racks. But it was too late. Sharp crashes cried entire stacks of plates were gone... one... three... a cascade.

And *Conquest* kept listing.

Simultaneously two dozen ketchup bottles exploded on the tiles. Plates in hundreds shattered everywhere. I tripped over a plastic pitcher crushed open on the floor. In a blink the cream it held streaked fifty feet across the deck. Soon I had to hold something to avoid falling myself.

Then she righted. The chaos audibly lessened, but only for a moment. *Conquest* righted abruptly: too abruptly. Experienced crew members knew what that meant and abandoned efforts of protecting property in favor of protecting themselves. I gripped the buffet as the floor tried to dump me starboard. The cream, still very much alive, flashed a shocking white lightning bolt zigzagging into the dark. Watching the fluid move so violently made me realize there was something much greater to worry about.

A waiter was stationed by the pool. I had assigned him there just minutes ago!

I scrambled over the slanting deck to the stern with great difficulty; to the pizza station, the grill, the pool. A gaping, empty hole was all that remained of the pool, for all the water had already surged out to sweep across the restaurant. Knocking tables and chairs aside, the churning mass eased in volume as it drained en masse to the deck below. Left were unsecured tables piled high in a corner, entangled and dripping, legs worked together like the roots of a mangrove. Perched atop and soaked to the skin was a smiling Indonesian waiter.

A close call, but everyone was all right.

What had happened?

Conquest had nearly collided with an errant barge while entering the busy mouth of the Mississippi River. A late-night sinking in the vast, black wastes of the ocean, a la *Titanic*, it was not. But was sinking ten miles from the unlit, swampy, forested bayou really any better? Because the water was not one degree above freezing did not mean a better chance at survival, it meant you'd linger... terrified... struggling... until exhaustion took you down, down to the dark depths.

This, on a modern cruise ship equipped with the latest technology and every conceivable manner of communication. Should you be worried about ships hitting each other?

No. How many big ship to ship collisions have their been in the last century? In the modern cruising era, only the *Andrea Doria* was so doomed—and that was in 1956. In a foggy night near Nantucket she was struck broadside by the *MS Stockholm*. The *Andrea Doria* listed so badly that half her lifeboats were unusable. Despite this, her modern ship design was so efficient she remained afloat for eleven hours, allowing all survivors to be safely evacuated. That's less miracle and more engineering.

Miraculous was Linda Morgan. The teenager was sleeping in her cabin with her half-sister when the ships struck. The blow somehow lifted her into the bow of the *Stockholm* and deposited her safely behind a bulkhead... even as the ships scraped along each other through the fog. Later, she was found wandering around asking for her mother in her native Spanish, much to the astonishment of the Swedish-speaking crew. Alas, her sister in the next bunk was not so lucky, nor were 45 others directly struck by the collision.

But nowadays ships have even more safety features, including zillions of inflatable life rafts that deploy automatically. Listing won't stop them from deploying in multitudes. They don't need balance, they don't need electronics, and they don't need manpower. They only need physics. They can't go wrong. Neither can you, if you stay calm. So enjoy your cruise!

Crew Survival Training

Survival training is an amusing label for watching a few videos on watertight doors and garbage separation, followed by quizzes on how many kilojoules of energy each survivor on a life raft was allocated per day.

Still, the films are far from boring. These are shockers reminiscent of what one sees on graduation day of driving class. 'Blood Flows Red on the Highway' becomes 'Blood Flows Red on the High Seas.' There were simulations of sinking ships and drowning people more intense than even James Cameron's *Titanic*. Even better, fires burned the unwary, crowds trampled the weak, and pirates attacked everybody. My personal favorite was the watertight door slicing a cow's leg in two. That was cool.

After the gore fest we were led up to the open deck on the bow of *Majesty of the Seas*, which was brutally exposed to the tropical heat of May in Key West. A bright orange life raft waited upon the humming deck. Steps led up to a platform before its opening. Atop it waited a Dutch officer.

"Working at sea and serving our guests is a wonderful privilege," he said in a crisp accent, "and this privilege is earned by keeping their safety first and foremost on our minds. Here, you are not a cabin steward or a waiter or a singer or a cook: you are crew who safeguard the lives of our guests. That means lowering lifeboats and directing panicked people, it means man overboard training. It may even mean fighting pirates."

Aha! Mild-mannered art dealer by day, pirate-smashing

crime fighter by night. I always wanted to be a superhero. I'm cool with tights.

"Each of you will be certified as 'personnel nominated to assist passengers in emergency situations' according to the training objectives of the International Maritime Organization, Resolution A770. This includes basic first aid, survival craft basics, fire fighting skills, and human relationships training."

It all sounded so dreadfully serious. All I wanted to do was jump into the big bright thing that looked just like one of those inflatable bouncy ball things you see at parks and events and stuff. Nobody else seemed to make that connection. Excepting only myself and one Jamaican lady, the crew was entirely Asian. Few, if any, were tall enough to reach my shoulder. Perhaps the inflatable bouncy ball things weren't so common in, like, Papua New Guinea.

"Now," the Dutchman ordered curtly, "everyone into the raft!"

More and more bodies disappeared into the raft, like the old clowns-fitting-in-the-funny car gag. The officer kept me outside, however. At first I thought this horribly unfair, because I wanted to play, too. It did, however, allow me to review the life raft in some detail. It was a shockingly large thing, considering how it compressed so snugly into keg-sized canisters. The base was two thick black rubber tubes bent into octagonal shape, the top a highly visible orange tent.

Grunts and complaints and waves of heat rose from inside. I peeked over the shoulder of the officer, who glanced down emotionlessly at the squirming mass of flesh below him. Suddenly I wasn't so eager to join in the fun.

"Tomorrow this raft could save your life!" he shouted. "Imagine this raft rocking at sea for unending hours under the hot sun."

"It is under the hot sun!" someone shouted back.

Unperturbed, the officer continued, "This raft holds twenty-four crew and guests. There are currently only twenty-three crew inside. How does it feel?"

Angry mutterings and cynical jokes answered.

"That is correct," he agreed solemnly. "It is difficult to fit you all in."

I was motioned to approach. I stared with trepidation at the inside. Bodies were like sardines in a can. Those people crammed at the sides were neatly arranged, but the middle was a mosh pit. There were no bouncy balls to be seen whatsoever.

"I said this is for crew and guests," the Dutchman emphasized. "Now, what is the difference between each of you and the average American?"

Alarm bells went off in my mind when the officer placed his foot on my behind. "About one hundred pounds!"

I was launched into the air.

Through the whistling wind I heard someone cry, "Ahh! Big Mac attack!"

I landed atop the bodies with a crunch. This did not endear me to the crew. Groans rose as I crushed entwined legs and smashed into bodies. The hapless men writhed and squirmed to get out of my way. Laughter from those safe at the edges turned to hollers as the shock waves of my inglorious entry radiated outward, with elbows elbowing and knees kneeing. When all the hubbub died down, I wriggled into an awkward position atop four Indonesian and Filipino men and propped my back against the Jamaican woman.

"Now listen up," the Dutch officer continued. "As you can see, survival is about everyone. There is no room for anyone to focus solely on himself. You are all crew and obey, but can you imagine this raft filled with complaining guests? They are scared and do not know what to do, they may be separated from loved ones, and they certainly are not comfortable. Imagine this filled with Americans and not Indonesians!"

"Or da rats with ESP!" cried the Jamaican behind me.

The officer blinked slowly as the odd statement was processed. Finally, no doubt due to uncontrollable curiosity, the man asked, "Excuse me?"

The bold Jamaican shook her head with emphasis. A few braids smacked me in the face.

"Rats always leave da sinking ship first," she proclaimed. "I know for fact two ships in da south Carib sank and da rats left first. For fact! Now how dey know what's up? Dey gots da ESP, mon, and dey get in da raft!"

Things went downhill from there.

The Truth About Life Raft Survival

If your ship sinks and you're stranded, without food or water, with only an open boat and your own resources, can you stay alive?

Sure!

This was proven in rather dramatic fashion by Alain Bombard, who believed people could survive such trials. Of course, nobody else believed it, so it was up to him to prove it. Thus on October 19, 1953 the Frenchman voluntarily set off from the Canary Islands, alone. He intended to cross the entire Atlantic Ocean, from Europe to the West Indies, in an open-topped 15 foot rubber boat. Not a scrap of food. Not a drop of water. Just his clothes and an unshakable faith in his own theory. Oh, and an inflatable cushion.

Bombard believed that shipwreck survivors died drinking seawater simply because they waited too long to do so. From the time he set off, he drank 1.5 pints (.71 liters) of seawater every day. He supplemented this with water squeezed from fish caught with a makeshift harpoon.

Gross? Most definitely. But not as bad as the raw plankton he swallowed. He would trail a cloth through the sea to capture the microscopic organisms, figuring if they could keep a whale alive, then he'd have no problem. Unlike a whale, which can gobble zillions of the stuff with one big mouthful, he struggled to get one or two teaspoons of it a day. After twenty days of this self-induced torture, he broke out in a painful rash.

But he wasn't dead.

Not that the sea didn't try. A storm within days of setting out nearly wrecked his little rubber boat. His sail ripped and the spare was blown away entirely. More distressing still was what else it blew away: his inflatable cushion. Knowing he could live without food and water, but not without a comfortable posterior, Bombard secured his craft with a sea anchor and jumped overboard after it.

Mistake.

While he was diving, he discovered to his horror that the sea anchor was not working. This parachute-like device was tied to the boat and left to drag in the ocean, thus keeping the craft nearby. Without it, the current was sweeping the boat hopelessly out of reach. Luckily the sea anchor fixed itself—it had been caught in its own mooring line—and he was able to haul himself back aboard. Strangely, whether he retrieved the cushion or not was never revealed.

Weeks passed, but Alain Bombard did not die. He survived off of seawater, plankton, and whatever raw fish he could catch at the surface. On day 53—that's right, 53—he hailed a passing ship to ask his position. Sadly, he had another 600 miles to go before reaching his intended destination. He seriously considered giving up, for had he not already vindicated his supposition that man could survive on sea water? Indecision wracked the poor man.

After mulling it over, Alain decided to split the difference. He had a meal on the ship, then, joie de vivre revived, voluntarily returned to his little rubber boat. One wonders if he was able to procure another seat cushion.

On Christmas Eve he reached Barbados, having sailed more

than 2,750 miles (4425 kilometers) in 65 days. He lost 56 pounds (25 kilograms) and was supremely grumpy, but was otherwise fine. And that was in an open boat with nothing.

If your cruise ship goes down and you're in a life raft, it has a roof. That makes a huge difference. Also, life rafts are equipped with emergency rations of food and water, and even fishing kits. Most importantly of all, however, is that modern life rafts have radio transponders. You won't have to wait months. Probably not even days.

The moral of the story? If your ship goes down, don't panic. Be awesome. You absolutely have it in you.

It's just gonna taste really gross.

The Truth About Hiring Crew

Here's how to get a job on a cruise ship: persistence, bribes, and a lot of lies!

My Romanian girlfriend Bianca and I were sitting in the office of Ovidiu, the Romanian recruiting agent for Carnival Cruise Lines. He was a slender man with a handsome face, a very handsome wardrobe, and an extremely handsome office. His suite comprised the entire second floor of a brick building, featuring numerous windows looking into a lush interior court. Light filtered in through an angled glass skylight and past his mezzanine entrance, making it look like a bridge over a jungle.

"Americans can't handle ships," he said.

"So I hear," I replied, giving Bianca an amused look. She sat in the chair beside mine, looking relaxed but serious.

"What is it you think I can do for you?" Ovidiu asked. "I am a recruiter for Romanians, not Americans. There are no American recruiters, of course."

"So I hear," I repeated. "Why is that?"

"Because none apply," he replied thoughtfully, leaning back. "Why would you want to? The work is very hard, and the money is very small."

Bianca raised an eyebrow, and Ovidiu hastily added, "For an American."

"I'm not thinking big," I said. "It's just a waiter job. I've been in restaurants for a decade."

"Not on ships, you haven't," he pointed out. "Do you know

computers?"

"He knows computers," Bianca interrupted, before I could protest.

"Other than doctors, who are supernumeraries anyway, and entertainers, who have their own agencies, the only position I can even think of for an American would involve computers."

"I just want to be a waiter, man," I repeated.

Ovidiu leaned forward skeptically. "Why?"

"My reasons are irrelevant."

"No, they're not," Ovidiu insisted. "Why would they bother with someone who will just quit? They'll want to know your story before they even think of meeting you. And believe me, they'll need to meet you."

"I want to be with Bianca," I explained. "If we have the same job, we can be together. That simple."

"I see," he said, nodding. "Well, in my ten years at Carnival, I've never seen even one American. I would not even talk to you, but Bianca is a good employee and a friend. Again, what is it you think I can do for you?"

"You can think Romanian-style," Bianca answered for me. "Not American-style."

Ovidiu thought for a moment, frowning. "No, that won't work. The bribes are to convince me, and you don't need to worry about that. Really, Bianca, I would sign him on if I could. I can't."

He opened a drawer from his desk and pulled out a pack of cigarettes. We declined his offer, so he casually lit one for himself. He leaned towards me, elbows on the desk and asked, "You want to know why Bianca doesn't need to bribe me?"

"Suddenly I'm not so sure," I replied wryly.

"Bianca is the only one who almost beat me. Almost, of course."

I looked at Bianca, but she said nothing. Her delicate wiggle of satisfaction was corroboration enough.

"As agent to cruise ships, my job is to screen people. If I like them, and there is a job opening, I find the right place for them. Bianca applied for the restaurants. That's the highest paid job, so everybody applies for it first. It is also the toughest, so I don't let them by easily."

He paused, grinned, and offered Bianca a cigarette again. This time she accepted, leaning forward to accept the light with a creak of leather skirt.

"She said she worked at a certain restaurant. I called the owner and he said, 'oh, of course, she has worked here for years!' That, of course, only meant she could lie and bribe. Romanian-style. Turns out, she only volunteered there for a summer."

Bianca shrugged, explaining, "I needed to learn restaurants."

"I knew she was lying, but couldn't catch her. She was too smart. She had asked all of her waitress friends penetrating questions and listened close. I asked her this and that, and of her experiences here and there. She had an answer for all of it. The performance was amazing."

Bianca laughed, and added, "Until Ovidiu pulled his bloody secret weapon from the filing cabinet!"

Reflecting upon what I knew of Romanians thus far, I presumed this meant a large knife.

"A linen napkin," Ovidiu clarified. "I told her 'You said you know half a dozen napkin folds. Show me.' She wilted before my very eyes, like a Gypsy had spit in her ice cream. I told her to relax, go have a cigarette, then come back. I had her paperwork done by then."

"All that to be a waiter?" I asked. "It's not rocket science."

Ovidiu leaned back again. He casually blew his smoke into the air, then looked me in the eye.

"You have no idea what you're getting into, do you?"

You Dirty, Dirty Scoundrel, You

Some people go to great lengths to 'protect' themselves from cruise-borne germs. I'm not talking about the obsessive-compulsive disorder folks who have a legitimate obsession. I'm talking about the sheltered, paranoid freaks who no longer enjoy the benefit of healthy immune systems because they have utterly destroyed every bacterium on their persons with anti-bacterial gels, creams, and probably suppositories. Many a cruise guest enters his/her cabin and promptly wipes down every conceivable well-used surface with disinfectant wipes: light switches, door knobs, faucets, and telephone. Some go so far as to place the TV remote control in a quart-sized Ziploc bag.

I don't blame you, gentle reader. Take a few precautions to feel better. But rest assured, the ship crew has already done this. Every home port, room stewards disinfect every high touch item in the cabin, especially in the bathroom. That bathroom has about 400 times less bacteria than your office desk. But go ahead and wipe down that toilet seat again. Better yet, bring those disposable paper seats. Right?

Remember: cruise ships clean everything above and beyond what's required by land businesses. They're required to. Indeed, as a waiter I bleached restaurant and kitchen stuff daily until my fingers literally split open. Yes, we waiters bleach those menus, salt and pepper shakers, even backs of the chairs. Stewards bleach those elevator buttons and rails. If there does happen to be a virus outbreak on board, we double wash all plates, double wash all glasses, double wash all silver. Feel safer?

You shouldn't. Bwah-ha-ha!

Why do I taunt you thus? Because you, gentle germophobe, brought loads of bacteria with you. Take your toothbrush, for example. You put it in your mouth twice a day—or at least should. Yet your mouth contains billions of bacteria. According to WebMD, scientists have identified more than 700 different types of microbes in the average human mouth. Every ER doctor knows that bites from human mouths are vastly more prone to infection than those from animals.

But it's not just your own nastiness on your toothbrush. If you don't cap that wet toothbrush, you are potentially contaminating it by merely flushing the toilet—paper seat and all. Researchers discovered flushing the toilet sends a spray of bacteria and virus contaminated water droplets into the air. These float around a bathroom for at least two hours after each flush before landing on surfaces—like your toothbrush [University of Arizona Department of Soil, Water and Environmental Science].

What about the toiletries you brought with you? Ladies, how often do you disinfect every tube, handle, and applicator in your make-up bag? Guys, you bleachin' handles on those razors?

Fret not. You need bacteria to stay healthy. Why do you think babies put everything in their mouths? They're building up their immune systems! The paranoia of all-things-filthy is predominantly a First World trait. We are relentlessly barraged by advertising for cleaning products. It's gone overboard. Why, even Healthline's website spread the alarm that washed laundry left unattended in a machine, even a few minutes, is like "the fertile crescent for germs."

That's right, even cleaning things isn't enough! Wrap yourself in cellophane right now or you're doomed!

All joking aside, if you have a compromised immune system, please to take extra precautions. But sensible precautions suffice for most of us. I worked on ships four years and never got sick once, and much of that was when malnourished and utterly sleep-deprived. I survived countless norovirus outbreaks without incident. Am I made of sterner stuff? Most certainly not. Just ask my ex-wife. No, I just made sure I washed my hands properly. Note the emphasis.

For the real culprits are our own bad habits. For cryin' out loud, wash your hands after using the toilet and before you eat. You'd be shocked how few people actually do that. According to research conducted for the American Society for Microbiology in 2005, even among those who claim to always wash their hands after using the bathroom, they actually only do so 83% of the time. Before eating or handling food it's only 77%, and the number drops alarmingly from there. After petting a dog or cat it's as low as 42%, and after coughing or sneezing only 32%. After touching money? Only 21%. What blows my mind is that after changing a diaper the number is only 73%! You'd think people would get that one right. Again, those are numbers from those who think they wash their hands all the time.

Even if you do wash your hands, do you do it properly? You've seen TV shows where the surgeon scrubs and scrubs and scrubs all the way up to his elbow. You don't need to go that far, but you need to use that soap for enough time to let it do its work. On *Conquest*, the captain even had to publicly humiliate himself by singing "Happy Birthday" to himself on the PA system to drive home how long you should soap those hands. The CDC even says hum it twice.

The best thing, of course, is sterilization from the inside out: down some shots of booze. Helps with a great many issues.

Was Carnival Triumph the Grossest Ship Ever?

The *Carnival Triumph* safely returned to port after an ordeal at sea. I'm happy to say that, during the intense media coverage on CNN, BBC, and other networks—which I was reluctantly a part of—passengers unanimously praised the tireless hard work and positive attitude of the crew. There were loads of horror stories about poor sanitation on the crippled ship. Why, surely it must have been hundreds! In fact, there were only a handful of people who actually reported such issues, but sensationalist reporting is hot as ever.

Alas, the really nasty stuff is not specific to disaster. Allow me to share a particularly gross ship I worked on for months...

Gross things are common on cruise ships. No, not the gastronomic atrocities occurring nonstop at the buffets—horrifying as that may be to quantify—but what lies below the waterline. No, not the slimy, oil-tainted waters of the bilge, either. I'm talking about what life is like on the crew decks.

When *Carnival Triumph* made the news in early 2013, it was because a fire left it without propulsion, little running water, less electricity, and bereft of sanitation. One passenger reported "sewage running down the walls and floors" and said travelers were being asked to defecate in bags and urinate in showers because toilets weren't functioning. This was understandably shocking, considering how rarely passengers endure such privations. The crew deal with it every day. It should be noted they bring it on themselves.

Crew are generally denied food in their cabins because it invariably ends up in the toilets in a most nonbiological manner. Hiding evidence of a smuggled, late night snack is always the same: flush it. After all, there are no portholes twenty feet below the sea. But ship toilets are very, very sensitive. The crew? Not so much.

Oddly enough, this disposing of contraband was the only time many flushed the toilets at all. This can be partly explained by the wide variety of nationalities that compose the crew. Hygiene standards vary radically from nation to nation, but can be all but absent in some developing nations. Such is the resource pool from which the cruise industry hires its labor.

When first indoctrinated into crew, on day one, everyone is educated on what is required for first-world hygienic standards. They are ordered to wash daily and to use deodorant, whether they 'need' it or not. Many even comply. But when working a minimum of eighty hours a week without a day off for ten months straight, focus flags.

When working on Royal Caribbean's *Majesty of the Seas*, fish bones backed up the sewage system so often that the entire aft crew deck smelled like feces. Literally. And this was where the crew kitchen and dining room were located! Imagine, if you will, standing inside an overflowing pit latrine—old school, mind you, not a modern port-a-potty with chemical air fresheners. Now imagine, if you dare, eating a roast beef sandwich inside it. I was pretty thin in those days....

On *Majesty of the Seas*, crewmen—for they were invariably men—lived in tiny, shared cabins along the main corridor leading to the crew mess. Tucked between were communal showers and toilets. Everything was crowded, everything stank. And it was stiflingly hot. Because the cooling system was also spotty, all doors were always open. Three times a day, on the way to every meal, I passed dozens of overworked zombies brushing their teeth beside toilets filled to the brim, lids wide open. A perfect appetizer for a enjoying a meal in a latrine.

I learned about such things in dramatic fashion upon signing onto *Majesty* as a junior officer. After returning to my cabin, I discovered a man wearing officers' whites bent over my desk, examining the contents. While there was no pretext of privacy on a cruise ship, having my own cabin had given me delusions of it.

Upon hearing me enter, the man shoved the drawer shut and irritably snapped, "Cabin inspection. I have reports that you routinely order room service. This is highly improper and will not continue. We have a cockroach problem in the stern deck, and I will not have it spread into this section of the ship."

I didn't have time to explain that I had just arrived because he brushed me aside to search my shower. Because cabin inspections were conducted by each department head and, since I was a department head, I suddenly realized the man searching my toilet was the most powerful officer beside the captain himself! He dropped the toilet lid with a slam, trying to hide his disdain behind a professional countenance. His grimace worked through.

"No fish bones," I said cheerily. He glared at me and replied, "I am seeking a shoe."

"Um... shoes?" I asked, confused.

He corrected me sharply, "A shoe! The entire sewage

system is backed up ship-wide because a crewman flushed a shoe down the toilet this morning."

Are You Cheap?

Do you ever wonder if you are merely cheap or actually a horrible person? Tipping is highly variable from culture to culture, and even gratuity-savvy passengers are lost at sea on cruise ships. What tips are expected, what's appropriate, what's… 'normal'?

Confusion surrounding this issue was intentionally created by the cruise lines themselves. The open secret is that the majority of staff is paid hardly anything at all. Cruise lines hide this behind gratuities. Especially with the rise to prominence of Carnival Cruise Lines—catering to overwhelmingly American and, thusly, gratuity-expectant guests—cruise lines realized they can get a whole lot more staff for a whole lot less money. This wage model was adopted by nearly every major cruise line, in many ways fueling the explosive growth of the industry throughout the 80's and 90's. Prior to that, cruising was exceptional and reserved for the well-to-do. Now it's a common vacation open to anyone budget-minded.

When I was a waiter on Carnival, my monthly salary was around fifty bucks (US $50). That's for working 12-15 hours a day, seven days a week. Tips kept me alive. True, tips added up to less than the U.S.'s average minimum wage, but that's a completely different subject.

Ah, but how much to tip? Even tip-savvy passengers had no basis from which to quantify their appreciation. In America, 15% gratuity is standard for acceptable service, 20% for good service. But on ships, individual meals were not broken down so numerically. So what's 20%?

Carnival eventually created automatic gratuities for passengers to opt in on for the whole cruise. Waiters knew any passenger who opted out of this service, whatever their reason, invariably skimped on tips. We hated those people. They almost never tipped enough. Especially in my case, because I was a terrible waiter.

Over time, some services became auto-tipped and others not. Yet every crew member was clamoring for tips, even those without any reason whatsoever for getting any (read: maitre d's). And what about room stewards, who had no inferred costs for their services? Well-intentioned passengers were confused all over again.

Cruise lines used this confusion to their advantage. A great example of this comes from P&O Cruise Lines. Prior to 2012, their managing director Carol Marlow was promoting P&O's value-for-money by pointing out that unlike some of its competitors, their company did not automatically add tips. Then, in April 2012, P&O began requiring auto-tips of £3.10 per person, per day. To explain the complete reversal, Marlow said, "Tipping has always been an integral part of the cruise experience but sometimes our passengers tell us they've been confused over whether or when to leave a cash tip for their waiters and cabin stewards. Our new tipping policy aims to remove this confusion in much the same way as most restaurants these days add a suggested gratuity to the bill." In other words, they flopped because the passengers were annoyed with their shallow efforts to appear a 'better deal'.

Nowadays, the majority of cruise lines 'take care' of their

staff with mandatory tipping. Good! If and when a cruise line offers pre-paid gratuities—and you have a soul—do it. Concerns about the line failing to properly distribute the money are rising, but that's step two. Step one is getting the cash out of the hands of us passengers. We all know how good ships are at that!

The best thing, of course, would be for cruise lines to remove tipping entirely. Basic wages should be enhanced to reflect that and the cost built into the basic price of a cruise. Crew could rely on a regular, guaranteed income. We've all had to slave away for absolutely no money at one time or another due to bad service completely outside our own arena. Plus it's easier on guests because tips are a hidden cost.

Desserts

Sweet nothings to leave you feeling happy.

Cuisine,
Conchs,
Birds,
& Embarrassments

How does cruise ship cuisine compare to the past?

Titanic Dining

1912, North Atlantic Ocean
1952, Trianon Palace Hotel, Versailles
2012, Lake Las Vegas

What do these three locations have in common? A sunken unsinkable ship. Duh.

We'll all heard of the ill-fated *R.M.S. Titanic*. We all know she was built for the super-rich, having the most elegant designs, the newest technologies, the oldest wines, and Europe's finest chefs. We've all seen the movie—unless you're a heartless communist. (Just kidding). Many of us know the immortal names associated with *Titanic*, such as Captain E.J. Smith or passengers John Jacob Astor and—everybody's favorite—Unsinkable Molly Brown. But few of us know that we can still enjoy a taste of *Titanic*. Yes, even us mere mortals on a budget.

Titanic was an Olympic class ocean liner featuring only the finest luxuries and opulence. The rich wood-paneled B-Deck Café Parisian and D-Deck Dining Saloon were focal points, offering the finest cuisine for the First Class passengers prepared by the Emeril Lagasses and Gordon Ramseys of the day. Of the 3,547 passengers on the maiden voyage, 416 First

Class passengers paid the equivalent of US$124,000 to experience the finest, most elegant, most luxurious, most whatever—choose your own superlative—dining experience the world had to offer. Sadly, the diners went down with the ship. Happily, the recipes did not.

In 1952 the father and son chefs of the Trianon Palace Hotel in Versailles recreated items from the doomed liner's famed menu. Their grandson listened on as they discussed the planning, preparation, and service to the guests at the Trianon.

"I have never forgotten," recalls the now third-generation Chef E. Bernard. "I have always remembered tales of the *Titanic* Dinner prepared by my father and grandfather in Versailles... and I have dreamed of following in their footsteps by offering such a unique dining experience here, too."

Chef E. Bernard's vision has now become reality. "Diner du *Titanic*" (to dine on the *Titanic*) is a weekly offering at his lakeside Bernard's Bistro Restaurant Lake Las Vegas. The desert wastes mere miles from where 119 nuclear bombs were set off may seem an odd—if not impossible—location to rekindle oceanic glory. Never underestimate Vegas, baby.

Starting at seven bells shipboard time (7 p.m. for others), those booking passage at Lake Las Vegas will be given a White Star Line "Boarding Pass" and offered an unhurried evening of sumptuous epicurean dining. Music of the day will be played on piano, violin and guitar—recreating the same make-up of musicians that played aboard the *Titanic*. Various special decorative touches will help complete this bygone shipboard ambience and elegant dining experience.

The first menu of the *Titanic* dining series offered dishes drawn from the actual First Class menu on the ship's maiden voyage. While the menu varies from week to week, each meal is based on actual dishes either served aboard *Titanic* or those prepared by world-class chefs for the White Star Line sister-ships, the *R.M.S. Olympic* and *R.M.S. Britannic*.

For the full experience, I recommend first taking the *Titanic* tour at the nearby Luxor casino in Las Vegas, where you can see actual artifacts plucked from the ocean's depths. You'll be immersed in the moment far more than you thought possible. Why, they even give you a boarding pass from an actual passenger of the ill-fated cruise. Only at the end, after being awed and astonished by the luxury, then crushed by the tragedy, will you discover whether or not 'you' survived.

For those intimidated by a lavish five-course meal, Chef Bernard offers an elegant three-course alternative. Each seating begins with a glass of champagne, followed by the European-style gourmet dinner courses, and finally ends hours later with fabulous pastries prepared from the actual pastry recipes of the *Titanic's* First Class dining room.

The full meal costs only $65 per person, or $45 for the lighter fare. Better yet, there is no chance whatsoever in hell of encountering an iceberg—not even in Las Vegas. Nor is anybody firing off nuclear weapons anymore, either. You simply can't go wrong. Unless you are sidetracked by the roulette wheel, of course.

By the way, a First Class menu from the *Titanic's* last lunch was auctioned in 2012 for $117,320. Kept by a prominent San Francisco banker named Washington Dodge—after being found in the purse of his wife, who survived the tragedy—it was dated

April 14th, 1912 and featured several courses, such as eggs Argenteuil, consomme fermier and chicken à la Maryland.

What's your most embarrassing crew moment?

The Worst Striptease Ever

My last cruise as a waiter on *Carnival Conquest* was one to remember. My section was filled with twenty coeds just graduated from college: all 22, brainy, and beautiful. These women wanted to party and indulge in every aspect of the Fun Ships they could. This meant lethal flirting with their hapless waiter. I was in heaven.

At the end of the first dinner, my ladies remained long after. They asked a flurry of questions, 'Are you single?' 'Can you party with guests?' 'Show us your cabin!' The question that got me in trouble, however, was unexpected.

'Why don't you dance during dinner like the other waiters?'

"I'm management next cruise," I explained. "They don't want me looking like a fool in front of staff I'll be in charge of."

"A convenient lie," they chastised.

"Convenient? Oh, yes," I agreed. "But not a lie."

"No fair!" they cried. "We want you to dance for us!"

"Only if you dance for me," I retorted.

The gauntlet thrown, all twenty rose and I was surrounded by spinning, whirling, and gyrating bodies. I looked on helplessly, realizing I was surely to be out-done by these women. "Come on! Join us!"

Realizing they wouldn't take no for an answer, I jokingly

countered, "I won't do dinner dances, but I'll do one better. My last day as a waiter, I'll do a striptease."

Their applause indicated my jest was not taken as such.

Serving the graduates was not work, but pleasure. They displayed patience for all things barring wine service. We laughed and flirted shamelessly. All week they had tried to kiss me in the dining room. The kiss became a game for us all, a silly little prize that both sides refused to relinquish. The challenge was spearheaded by a pretty lass named Jessica.

The final night came, then reluctantly drew to a close. The party was over, and I would miss serving these very fun ladies. Yet they remained to finish their wine. Neighboring stations emptied, leaving us a solitary island of gaiety.

"Last night!," Jessica called. "Where's our strip tease?"

All twenty cheered and began chanting, "Strip! Strip! Strip!"

"I can't," I replied lamely, fishing for an excuse, "I would need a stage. And there's no music."

"Regina!" they cried to my neighboring waitress. Though busy readying for the morning, one table had been forgotten and was completely empty. Only then did I realize it had not been forgotten at all—it had been reserved. Regina yanked the table cloth free to reveal an ideal stage.

"But there's still no music," I observed gratefully. Smirking, Regina signaled a hostess and suddenly "I'm Too Sexy" blared through the restaurant at tremendous volume.

I had been set up, but good.

Sometimes you gotta do what you gotta do.

I leapt onto the table and began a bad dance, whipping off

my bow tie and flinging it around my head. With surely the
most awkward moves ever witnessed, I flung off my vest and
began unbuttoning my shirt. Cheers roared from the graduates.
Applause echoed from waiters. Hostesses leered. Chanting to
the beat rose from everywhere.

Then the maitre d' entered the room.

I stopped mid-swing, stunned. But the coeds were just
getting started. They rushed from their seats to yank me off the
table. Hands tore at my chest. Buttons popped out, flying in all
directions. My shirt was half ripped off before I could stop it. I
had heard that women got far wilder then men at strip clubs, but
this was ridiculous. Why, I even felt my belt slipped free!
Quickly I gripped my pants before they were yanked down.

I began bellowing, not unlike some elephant seal under
attack. Alas, there was no denying the authority of dozens of
red-tipped fingernails. Here I was living my fantasy since
puberty, yet was fighting like mad!

One would think the action would stop with the approach of
the maitre d'. One would be wrong. He just grinned and let it
flow, reserving the moment for future blackmail.

Do passengers ever misbehave?

When Passengers Attack!

People can be annoying. When on vacation—especially on a cruise ship far from home—they can be even more annoying. What happens at sea, stays at sea. Perhaps some people figure anonymity makes rude behavior OK. Perhaps some people are just so relaxed, or so centered on their hard-earned focus on self, they let little things slide. Perhaps some people are just assholes.

I vote the latter.

Sometimes guests misbehaving is small. The most annoying thing I recall from my four years working on cruise ships was quite small. I think that's why it grated me so much: sometimes a surprise, light strike hurts worse than a heavy blow. Just ask any man who's been hit below the belt!

As an auctioneer, I had arranged the surface of my desk with all manner of flyers, pamphlets, and books. I got it all ship-shape, as they say, arranging stacks to perfection. The task took only about five minutes but made me feel comfortable and organized, ready for action. The first lady that walked up plunked her gargantuan bag right atop the desk with so much force that books tumbled to the floor and papers scattered into every corner of the corridor. She wanted directions to the gangway.

How rude!

Some guest misbehavior is just opportunistic. Again as an

art auctioneer, I was targeted for freebies. A power cord taped to the deck had come partially loose near the wall. A little old Asian lady made a bee-line for the far side of the thirty-foot wide corridor and 'tripped'. That is, she had a misstep, because she only pretended to trip. I saw her through the entire pantomime. She made a fuss. I apologized. After fixing the loose cord, I thought the matter closed.

That night—at 11 p.m., I might add—I was called into the hotel director's office. There waited the little old Asian lady and her daughter. They had declared their intent to sue the cruise line for being racist. The hotel director had pointed out how absurd that was, considering 60 nationalities worked together on that very ship, so she instead intended to sue me personally.

Using her daughter to translate—despite having spoken clear English to me earlier—she claimed that had she been white, I would have treated her better after her 'fall'. Via daughter-translator, she called me a racist to my face. I usually laugh off verbal barbs, but that time I was not amused. I went off on her—much to the chagrin of the hotel director—yelling that I had even dated an Asian woman.

All charges were dropped.

But some guest misbehavior is so egregious that it spawns nothing short of hatred. As a waiter, one particular family was so over-the-top gluttonous and selfish that my poor assistant literally had an emotional breakdown in the dining room. It was the most awful thing I'd ever seen in my life.

Whatever the reason for guest misbehavior, it's usually best to not let it bring you down, whether cruising as passenger or crew. Because, when official policy is stirred, the finger of blame rarely points where it should. Take the sinking of *Costa Concordia*, for example, off the coast of Italy. While this tragedy was entirely and utterly the fault of the idiotic and indefensibly cowardly Captain Schettino, Carnival Cruise Lines officially blamed passengers for all the internal damages to the *Costa Concordia*.

Aggrieved passengers, relatives of the deceased, and crew-members filed a lawsuit against the company. Carnival Cruise Lines refuted everything, filing court documents that state: "travelers' negligent or careless behavior were between the causes, if not the only cause, of the alleged injuries and damages." That's right: the drowning of 32 innocent victims was used to justify an insurance claim so a billion dollar corporation could save some money.

Are any cruise ships haunted?

Eternal Stowaways

"I saw a ghost."

"Mm hmm," I replied.

"Really, mate!" Rick insisted.

I looked up from my magazine, waiting casually for the flood of profanity sure to follow. I need not wait long.

"A bloody, f@*#ing goddamn ghost!" he continued.

His brow furrowed deeply and he stared at the galley deck. I was about to mock him, but chose instead to bite my tongue. Rick was shaking his head slowly back and forth, eyes staring at the floor... staring at nothing. With all those curls piled so high on his head, he reminded me of a fuzzy cat watching a tennis match on television. He was truly distraught. It was very late—I was only in the galley because my evening art auction ran exceptionally late—but I sensed he was too agitated to retire.

"You're serious?" I said.

It wasn't really a question. Of course he was serious. Rick was serious about everything that didn't matter. Had this been an issue of business, safety, or protocol—not that the latter matters too much—Rick would have been flighty and distant, if not downright disdainful. But things that implied secrets, cover-ups, conspiracies, and knowledge beyond the ken of man? Oh, Rick was serious about those, all right.

"I'm not biting," I replied, returning to my magazine.

"I really did," Rick mumbled quietly.

Quietly? Rick was never quiet. Even when he was performing a massage—he was the spa manager—he wouldn't shut up. Made a babbler like me seem mute. Now I was paying attention. Rick continued to stare at the floor, back and forth, back and forth.

"I saw it last night, too," Rick continued. "But I wasn't sure. I'd been hearing stories from Natalie for weeks, but blew them off. She drinks too much…"—he ignored my snort of derision —"…but then Claudia said she saw something, too. And now I have."

"In the spa?" I asked, now intrigued. The spa was deep in the bowels of *Wind Surf*, down near the waterline, back near the marina. At night it was a very quiet, very lonely place. Strange that such a small ship utilizing every cubic inch had locations that felt… well, abandoned. Everything was clean and tidy, of course, but I'd always felt that hallway to be somehow… different.

"I've noticed things moving behind the desk a lot," Rick said. "Hard to tell when bloody f@*#in' staplers move on their own when you have four employees, though. But you know the melon slices we keep in the urn of drinking water? I heard a gurgle or something and looked up in their direction. In the blink of an eye—in the blink of a bloody eye—they vanished! Then—splat! Right in front of me, right in the middle of the desk, the melons reappeared. Soaked all my paperwork and everything. Bloody f@*#in' weird, if you ask me. But even that wasn't enough to convince me the spa was haunted. Not 'til now.

"I was doing paperwork. It was about midnight. A bloody

f@*#in' guest walked right past me. I saw her clearly as she passed. Middle-aged, long brown hair, and a T-shirt that made her look chunky. I told her we're closed for the night, but she just walked through the spa and into Natalie's massage room. I followed right behind her, calling out. I was angry, actually, because I've had a bad time with stupid passengers complaining all bloody f@*#in' day. I was going to give this lady a piece of my mind. When I got to Natalie's room I flipped the light switch on... and nobody was there!"

Rick was clearly shaken. While he and I had had some pretty knock-down, drag-out fights about whether or not UFO's were parked in the center of the Earth—coming and going through the holes at the north and south poles, Rick insisted—I sensed he was genuinely scared. This, from a former Australian special forces operative who'd been in the middle of genocidal atrocities in East Timor.

In fact, *Wind Surf* had more resident ghosts than merely in the spa. The cruise director and shore excursion manager both swore they'd seen an apparition floating in the hallway outside the purser's office, mid-ship. The specter was a shadowy, yet overt, outline of a man from the waist-up. Both knew instinctively it was male, though no features could be seen on the hazy head. Both had offices with doors open to the haunted hall. Several times while doing paperwork in their respective offices on different occasions—though always late at night—they had sensed someone approaching their office. Looking up and out into the hall, they'd be shocked to see only half a man. Once spotted, the unbidden guest always faded back into the dark.

Not so with the purser, however. The Filipina had run to her office to retrieve copy paper for a busy purser's desk. It was in the middle of the afternoon, sunlight streaming through her office window to flood the hall. Arms laden with said reams, she rushed out of the office and ran smack-dab into the phantom.

She shrieked, at first thinking she had accidentally run into a crewman. But it wasn't a crewman—or at least none from the present. A caucasian man of average height regarded her skeptically... then vanished in a blink. The whole scenario happened so fast that, when pressed by the others, she couldn't answer if she had seen his legs or not.

"But he seemed quite real, quite solid," she stated resolutely. "I looked into his eyes. I saw surprise and something else... a sense of hopelessness. Though it was sunny in the hall, it felt very gloomy, very sad."

What's the weirdest thing you've seen at sea?

Gross Anatomy: G-rated

The anatomy of a conch is a curious and unnerving thing.

"Yeah, mon," said the Bahamian in the conch shack by the sea. "Take da skin and eyes right off, den trow dem in da water. Dey live by demselves for two more days."

My friend Laureen leaned over the counter to get a better look. In Donny's hands was a large conch shell and a knife.

"No, uh, gills or organs or anything?" I asked. "Just the skin? Living?"

Donny demonstrated. Experienced fingers pulled from the shell a floppy, purplish alien-slug-thing. Using his knife, he expertly cut something slimy off of something else slimy—conch skin and eyes from conch body, presumably—then tossed it over his shoulder. Through the open rear of the shack it flew, to plop back into the Caribbean Sea.

Donny was a thick man of middle years. The majority of his hair was going grey, and the majority of his teeth were going away. He and his wife, Monique, were proprietors of The Burning Spot, one of a long row of conch shacks lining a pier nestled beneath the huge bridge leading to Paradise Island.

The Burning Spot was the size of a garden shed, though the entire back was open to the sea. From the ceiling dangled all sorts of oddities mixed in with daily use items. Funky ornaments made of seashells swung in the breeze, bumping into grill brushes and spatter guards. The front wall of the shack folded into a counter, over which Laureen and I draped ourselves, beside a pile of conch shells strung together and heaped several feet high. As we watched Donny continue to intimately manipulate the conch, I pressed into the stack of conch shells.

"Gaaaaah!" I suddenly bellowed, stumbling backwards.

Laureen teased me with a voice usually reserved for small children, "Was it all slimy and icky, Bri Bri?"

"I-I just got tentacled!" I protested. "These things are still alive!"

Donny and Monique laughed hysterically. Monique even buried her face into his broad shoulder, overcome with mirth.

"If their skin can stay alive for two days," Laureen observed, poking me. "Whatcha think a whole one can do?"

I muttered, "I thought they were just shells. For decoration."

"Decoration's over dere, mon," Donny said, gesturing above him with his dripping knife. In the sheltered corner hung an old and tired pom pom, heavy and limp, some strands stuck to a cast iron pan. There was obviously a story there, but I wasn't sure I wanted to hear it. Watching Donny laugh maniacally holding a sharp knife in one hand, and a slain alien in the other, brought to mind all sorts of B-rated horror movie imagery.

"Donny catch dem every mornin'," Monique said.

"Cheerleaders?" I quipped, eyeing the pom pom dubiously.

Monique laughed heartily, revealing huge, brilliant teeth.

"He wish! He jump right off da back here sunup. Dey come

to da pier every day, like da ships."

Donny's continuing work freaked me out. From the bodies of the conchs he pulled weird, half toothpick-sized slivers of what looked like gelatin. Each such find brought delight, and he promptly popped them in his mouth. He loved 'em. I didn't have the stomach to ask if they were conch anatomy or parasites.

Yet despite the grisly performance, the results were worthy. We took our bowls of chilled conch salad to a crooked wooden table in front of the shack, and readily devoured the contents. The minutes-fresh meat was firm and bright. Mixed in were chopped tomatoes, onions, and peppers, the whole doused in copious amounts of freshly squeezed lime juice, then a pinch of salt and pepper.

The conch salad was delicious.

What's the weirdest thing you've seen in lost & found?

Gross Anatomy: PG-13

Lost and found issues happen all the time, to all of us, probably because as humans we have minds as tight as a sea sponge. Of course, you can always blame the cabin steward. Not for stealing, of course—that would be rude—but for leaving doors open while cleaning on embarkation day. It's not unheard of for someone to walk into the wrong cabin. Clothing will be put in the wrong closet and whatnot—and that's before they hit the drink specials on the Lido deck! Many times tip envelopes from the previous cruise will have been left on a cabinet. I'm happy to report that the only people who handle these more honestly than the crew are the passengers themselves. But I'm not talking about such mundane mysteries, oh no.

Though I've held several positions on cruise ships over the years, purser was not one of them. Lost & found is their purview and not something they are encouraged to discuss. They do a remarkably good job of that, too… especially when it counts. I knew a hotel director once who intentionally left his Rolex on a random deck just to check if lost items were flowing in the proper direction. He chose an hour when only crew were on board, of course—he's not stupid. While he expressed no outwardly visible sign of relief at finding his watch waiting in the lost & found, I secretly wonder if that's because several of us happened to be watching.

But as good as stewards are at depositing found items, and as good as pursers are at securing them, neither can resist sharing some of the more... colorful... items.

Some lost items are just too curious a mystery to not discuss. Like how could someone leave their false teeth beneath the bed? You'd think they would be missed. Less surprising, but still curious, was the huge Bowie knife left on a bed. How that even got aboard is a marvel. Or why was a lonely .22 caliber rifle cartridge in the bathroom sink? Same could be said for the bag of marijuana and accompanying pipe. Some abandoned items are less interesting and just plain rude, such as the used Depends found on a Holland American ship.

I sense that some items are lost because their owners secretly wanted to abandon them. Take the woman's thong found on *Sensation*, for example. Nothing unusual about that, other than that it was stuffed inside a sock and hidden beneath the shelves in the closet. And let us not forget the abandoned string bikini built for a woman of extraordinary proportions: she must have surely been 300+ pounds. I think everybody's glad she lost that, lest she actually wear it in public.

But the good stuff? That happened on *Wind Surf.*

Wind Surf is very small by modern cruise ship standards—only 14,700 tons—but is in fact the world's largest sailing vessel. With less than 200 crew aboard and no home port—we hopped from nation to nation in a way none of the big ships do —we all knew each other intimately. So small was *Surf*, in fact, that everybody wore multiple hats. Thus when helping out the front desk I became privy to the most wonderful lost & found item ever: a ten-inch long, glossy black dildo.

Juana, a petite young Filipina from a small village on a small island, had never seen anything like it. In fact, she didn't even know what it was. When its function was carefully explained to her by the flamboyantly gay French hotel director, her face turned beet red. He shared with me a sly grin, obviously enjoying himself immensely.

"What do we do with it?" Juana asked breathlessly.

"Nothing," the hotel director replied. "It stays in lost & found until it's claimed."

"Claimed...?" she asked. "You mean someone would actually call the cruise line and ask for it back?"

"Not likely," he agreed. "But protocol is protocol. Wait four weeks, then you can get rid of it."

The next month poor Juana was teased mercilessly. The innocent query of 'Did anyone claim it yet?' would bring about ferocious flushing of her pretty cheeks. She was just too cute to not tease. While discussions of the item were frequent, requests to see it were not... with one notable exception.

Yo Yo, the little Indonesian photographer—astoundingly younger and smaller than even Juana—was mesmerized. He lingered around the purser's desk at all hours of day and night, hoping to sneak a peek at the mysterious treasure. Though exceptionally shy, his wonder overcame all. Noting that he was the ship's photographer, I asked him why he didn't take a picture of it. He blushed as badly as Juana.

Eventually the allotted four weeks elapsed. Everybody wanted to know what Juana planned to do with the object of such endless conjecture. Upon asking her, I was a bit disappointed when she murmured it had 'disappeared'. I figured that was simply her way of dismissing an embarrassment. That is, until Yo Yo walked by and gave her a nod and a slight smile. Rather than meet his gaze, she looked down at her hands. She tried to cover her wrist absently.

"New watch?" I said, noting her subconscious reaction. Then I teased, "Or did that come from the lost & found, too?"

Juana snatched her hand away immediately and blushed furiously. Only later did I realize why the watch looked familiar: it was Yo Yo's! Methinks *Wind Surf* was home to some behind-the-scenes bartering.

What's the most amazing thing you've seen on ships?

The Bird Whisperer

I'm talking about a man of a different sort entirely. A bird whisperer. The Bird Man of *Conquest*. I prefer the latter name because it evokes the cramped, sparse living conditions of Alcatraz. That's closer to a crew's experience than, say, comfy suburbanites with enough expendable income for professional pet counseling. I'm not judging, but rather reminding that American attitudes towards animals are puzzling to the majority of the world. American pets are part of the family, receiving the same affection and accommodations as our children. Certainly my cats do!

But many people around the world coexist with animals in a way I can scarcely conceive. I saw some of it on *Conquest*.

We were docked in Montego Bay. The sun shot through the clouds in bold shafts and the air was heavy with moisture. Those of us in the Lido restaurant denied shore leave were consoled by the nearby presence of damp green tree tops, mottled with shadows, yet lively with colorful birds hopping to and fro. It was a quiet afternoon of dazzling beauty. Apparently we were not the only ones dazzled. A solitary bird, perhaps lured by the scent of food, had flown into the restaurant.

He was a small, gaily colored little bird. The poor guy fluttered about, unable to find the exit, confused by the overhanging mezzanine that refused to act like a jungle canopy. He zig-zagged through the dining room, zipping this way and that, growing more and more agitated by the minute. We gleefully kept the doors open and tried to herd him towards freedom. There was much laughter, but we were ultimately unsuccessful.

After a while, now flapping in pure desperation, the bird disappeared deeper into the galley. Suddenly we realized the little burst of joy that gave us a much-needed break in an otherwise rigid, exhausting routine had probably done so at the expense of his life. It was a sad moment.

"I'll get him," said a waiter confidently. He was from Indonesia. His name was Bambang.

"If he couldn't figure out how to escape through all these open double doors," I said doubtfully, "How can you expect to herd him through the small doors of the galley and the corridors?"

Bambang just smiled and asked, "May I go after him?"

Like I would say no. But then again, this could easily have been an excuse to sneak a cigarette while on duty. I've had waiters literally claim their mothers' death just to get an extra smoke. After Bambang disappeared into the galley, I shrugged and figured I'd not see him again that afternoon.

Nary five minutes passed and out from the galley came Bambang. We clustered around him, but he gave us a silent head-shake to keep us at bay. For perched upon his finger, tiny chest heaving, was the bird!

Bambang strode to the nearest exterior doors, whispering softly to his new companion. He even caressed it with gentle strokes of the back of his fingers. Once outside, the bird flew off to its native Jamaica.

"I'm from a small village in the jungle," Bambang explained simply before returning to soiled plates and silverware.

I was awestruck. Not just from his talent, but from the realization of how vastly different his home was than mine. Could I have made the transition Bambang had? Before ships he had not only been one with nature, but likely lived entirely defined by its caprice. How utterly different his life must have been before these tight metal walls, recycled air, and artificial light. I was reminded that each crew member, regardless of duties or labels, was indeed an individual treasure. And it gave me hope that I could maybe, just maybe, hope to someday control my cats.

Does the cruise have to end?

Cruise for Eternity

When you, dear passenger, step off the gangway for the last time, you are filled with a despondency that is barely tempered by the memories of good times. Why, oh why, you lament, does the cruise have to end? Ah, but it doesn't have to end! Now you can book a cruise that is the last you'll ever need to arrange. For you, the cruise will never, ever end. Indeed, it's for eternity. Cool, eh? Not really. You'll be dead.

My Final Cruise specializes in arranging details for those who have 'moved on' into the sea from cruise ships. Their website is most interesting reading.

Now, you will not be trussed in an old sail—the final stitch poked through your nose to ensure that you are, in fact, dead— and dumped overboard, where your body will sink slowly the long, long way down to the muddy ocean floor, there to be picked apart by large white crabs and other such detritus eaters. Nope, none of that good stuff. You're not a pirate, sorry to say. You'll be cremated long before any of that. My Final Cruise offers a selection of biodegradable urns, which is required by the International Maritime Organization. Prices range from $149 to $324 apiece, depending on your preferred style. After the ashes have been dropped overboard – which must be done outside of the 12-nautical mile limit – these special urns guarantee that the ashes will be dispersed in an environmentally friendly fashion, and that none of the ashes will wash up on the shore. Don't want to traumatize any swimmers, now.

The company sells receptacles pre-approved by the necessary bodies—pardon the pun—so you don't violate the strict oceanic policies regarding what can and cannot go overboard. The 'scallop shell' urn comes in three colors and costs $324.95. For cheap people such as myself, the simple 'locker' comes in six shades and costs an easy-on-the-funeral-budget $149.95. Of course, you have to book an actual cruise, so that's gonna run up the final cost. You'll probably save a lot on flowers, though, assuming you don't buy any on board. Most cruise lines will allow such crematory activity, but must be notified beforehand. This is not something you want to pop on the captain during a champagne meet and greet. My Final Cruise can book the entire cruise for you, via an affiliate cruise agent, so you don't have to mess with such pesky details. They can also arrange commemorative touches onboard, like a post-ceremony repast. Thus all you have to worry about is packing extra formal wear. The time of the ceremony depends on where the ship is—gotta be outside 12 nautical miles and, thusly, in international waters—and weather conditions. Under ideal circumstances, they say, it takes about seven minutes for the urn to sink.

The exact location where your ashes will be dropped is recorded in the site's database of funereal sites at sea. Via Google Earth, anybody can, uh, appreciate the location. The choice is yours whether to post a public obituary or just a simple 'X marks the spot'. As of 2012, the site only has two marked locations, one between South Carolina and Bermuda and another just north of Saint Martin. In fact, neither marker represents a real burial at sea site yet; they are merely samples. But the company hopes to be seeing lots of dead people in their world map soon. Don't we all.

Because of the waveblazing manner of their business, My Final Cruise has had to feel their way around a little bit. They had to brainstorm worst-case scenarios—wouldn't that be fun? —to build a solid reputation in a sensitive new industry.

"We don't want deaths being staged as part of a stag party or something," explains Abbie Sturdley of My Final Cruise. The company requires customers to provide them a death certificate, even though only the Bermuda Maritime Administration actually requires one. Strudley says attempts to partner with cruise lines, which they initially pushed for, were unsuccessful. "Because it's a sad occasion, lines don't really want to associate with it," she says. Still, as global environmental agencies tighten policies, she hopes that lines will start referring potential ash spreaders to My Final Cruise. I guess hope springs eternal!

About The Author

Adventuring in over 60 countries to gather material for his bestselling books, Brian David Bruns has won numerous literary awards, including the U.S. REBA Grand Prize. He has contributed to Yahoo Travel, BBC, CNN, Travel Channel, and Reader's Digest.

Bruns abandoned everything at age 30 to chase a woman who worked at sea, becoming the only American waiter in Carnival Cruise Line history to complete a full contract without quitting. His *Cruise Confidential* series chronicling the debacle has on two separate occasions been featured on ABC's 20/20.

After residing in Dracula's hometown for several years—a mere kilometer from the house where Vlad the Impaler was born—Bruns moved to Las Vegas with his Romanian wife. They live with two cats, Julius and Caesar.

Please enjoy the opening chapters from my latest nonfiction book, *Rumble Yell*. It won the Grand Prize from the U.S. Regional Excellence Book Awards and was also *ForeWord Magazine's* Humor Book of the Year. I hope that you, too, find it worthy. Do let me know!

Rumble Yell is dedicated to the men and women of our nation's military, both past and present. The book is about discovering the joys of small town America, which would not be possible without their sacrifices. As a small token of thanks and, perhaps, to remind them of what they're fighting for when far from home, I have donated over 1000 paperbacks to Operation Homefront and the Wounded Warriors Project.

Brian David Bruns
Twitter: @BDBauthor

Rumble Yell:
Discovering America's Biggest Bike Ride

Chapter 1: The Challenges

1

Why this place was chosen for 119 nuclear blasts was self-evident. Why I chose it for a bike ride was less clear. I was two hours away from the most revolting experience of my life, and I had no way of knowing it; a moment more awful than the 130° heat, more distressing than being alone in two million acres of utter waste. The nearest shade—a port-a-potty steaming in the sun—was twenty miles away. Getting there required a two-hour slog over desolate mountain ridges in unrelieved sun, on a bicycle so hot its metal burned any flesh unfortunate enough to touch it. My hands smarted even through gloves. No cars had passed this spot in days, barring a solitary DNR truck at 4 a.m. This I knew because I was already here in this horrible place. The truck's passage left a dead jackrabbit smashed upon the scalding asphalt at mile marker 33. Ravens circled above. They wanted me to leave. I wanted to leave.

But not before the most revolting experience of my life.

Training for the world's oldest, largest, and longest annual bike ride required some sacrifice. It was 500 miles of heat and hills and roadkill. Yet contrary to expectation, this greatest of Earth's bike touring tradition was not across the Sahara Desert, Australian Outback, or even somewhere in Europe. It was through America's heartland. I was training for RAGBRAI: [Des Moines] Register's Annual Great Bike Ride Across Iowa. That's right: Iowa.

I wasn't doing this for glory—one rarely associates glory with Iowa—nor, as seemed more likely, was this some form of self-flagellation. This was to reconnect with an old friend I hadn't seen in twenty years. Aaron was a fascinating guy. Barring a penchant for wearing kilts and a need for corrective lenses, he was the living incarnation of Indiana Jones. Any opportunity to converse with such a man was worth some effort, and to rekindle an old friendship was even better.

I rubbed the grit from my eyes and squinted to the heat-wavering horizon. He better be worth it!

2

I am not a bicyclist by nature. I hadn't ridden one since my youth, which was a depressing number of decades ago. When Aaron suggested riding RAGBRAI, I said yes before actually thinking it through. Fortunately I was fit, but in other areas entirely, like running or dodging household objects occasionally thrown by my wife. If I was going to safely ride 500 miles, it required planning. Training. Oh, and a bike. I needed one of those.

How does one plan for such a monumental ride? Fortunately, RAGBRAI wasn't America's biggest bike ride without a great body of knowledge to draw upon. The official website was loaded with advice, including a calendar of recommended training rides. In fact, mercifully little thought would be required. Just follow directions to avoid injury. Being married, I was well versed in following directions to avoid injury.

So training I could do. 1,000 advance miles? Twas nothing. Buying all the gear from scratch? Ha! Credit cards. This was looking easier by the minute. But there was one great challenge I feared insurmountable. No, not the heat of my home in Las Vegas, nor even finding time for 1,000 training miles therein. Something far, far more difficult awaited me: getting permission from my wife.

How to broach this adventure for the boys? Rare is the man who knows what women want to hear. This was compounded for me because my dear Aurelia was foreign. She grew up in the humble Romanian countryside but abandoned home for the action of the capital city. The result was a woman of ambition and self-reliance tempered by a natural shyness and her culture's enforced passivity in women. I just never knew when and where she would make a stand.

But what really made connection difficult, far more than her having lived under the Iron Curtain, was English. It was her third language and entirely self-taught by listening to hip hop music. Emigrating to Las Vegas did nothing to help get rid of her... colorful... phraseology. While I applauded Aurelia continually on this amazing feat of self-instruction, inwardly I cringed during even regular conversation. Her way of ordering me to the gym, for example, was by saying, "Junk in your trunk means no hoes 4 U."

Thus it was to this fitful little volcano I need explain my desire of riding RAGBRAI across my native state. Did I appeal to the fond pastoral memories of her youth, or work the 'everybody's doing it/hip today' angle? In the end I selected a different approach altogether. I decided to make it all about me.

Dangerous? To be sure. Foolish? No doubt. But it was honest. That had to count for something.

Thus I expounded upon how completing RAGBRAI was every Iowan's rite of passage, a quantifiable method of proving our worthiness of that greatest of honors: being Iowan. We're a proud, hard-working folk, I exclaimed, getting positively worked up over the awesomeness of laboring 500 miles over 'amber waves of grain'—Iowa's lack of wheat fields notwithstanding—until I began singing the national anthem. This did not improve my argument.

"You want that for vacation?" Aurelia squeaked dubiously in her mousy voice. "Imma be in Hawaii. That's America, too."

"Come on, you've been to Iowa to see family..." I began.

"Chillaxin' with ya homies is different," she replied. "Doncha wanna go somewhere interesting?"

"So you think Iowa's not worthy?" I chided.

Alas, Aurelia had a point. Did I really want to spend my vacation in Iowa? I was from Iowa, what more was there to see? After twenty-five years there, surely I'd seen it all—or all I wanted to, anyway. Since this wasn't about family, what on Earth would take me there, after all the exotic places I'd seen as a travel writer? A friend, that's what.

"We went to Maui last year," I protested. "You forced me to drive all over the island so you could see each and every beach, each and every town, each and every palm tree! I chauffeured you ten hours a day, every day. It was the most exhausting vacation I've ever had."

"And biking 500 kilometers is chill?"

"Miles," I corrected reflexively. "They're a lot longer than kilometers."

She batted her pretty eyelashes at me, revealing to my slow wits that I had just blundered into a trap.

"But... but... old people do it!" I blurted, desperate. "I mean retirees and stuff."

"Then bag her when you're old," she said, wiggling figure settling into a firm stance.

"There's pie," I tried.

"No pie," she said. "Denied!"

Unfortunately Aurelia also loved Suze Orman's TV show about finances. She delighted in the long list of callers asking Suze's advice, such as, "I'm worth $1.3 Million. Can I buy a new Prius?" Suze's answer never varied: denied! Aurelia's tiny voice somehow only underscored the finality of the word. But I had an ace up my sleeve. One of Iowa's triumphs was Aurelia's Achilles heel.

"They have pork."

She paused.

"Old school pork," I pressed on, sensing my advantage. "Heaps of it. Iowa pork chops are over a pound each, baby."

Despite my dinky wife's utter lack of body fat, she consumed vast amounts of pork. One might say freakish amounts of pork. Her metabolism was hyperactive, like that of a small mammal, and she regularly snarfed down more food than I, an active man double her weight. Further, she went straight for the heavy stuff. No lean tenderloins for her, oh no. Growing up in rural Romania she learned to dunk hunks of pork into barrels of bubbling, rendered pork fat. With salt. They ate entire slabs of smoked fat called *slanina*, sometimes mixing it with eggs but more often popping it straight into their mouths. With salt. While American bacon was little meat and lots of fat, Romanian bacon abandoned the idea of meat altogether. But had lots of salt.

"Iowa has the best pork in the country," I continued. "It's glorious, I tell you, glorious! Our pigs live the high life. I can bring some home."

"When you leaving?"

3

Of course Aurelia encouraged rekindling my friendship with an old high school buddy. Though Romanian, she wasn't a witch. But that didn't mean she gave me carte blanche, either. I was under strict orders to manage the budget such that Hawaii was still available later. I happily informed her that RAGBRAI meant camping, so the only cost was reasonably-priced vendor food all week. Oh, and transportation to Iowa. And buying a bike. And its transportation to Iowa. And, um, gear, like jerseys and bike shorts and a helmet. And a tire pump. And energy bars. Icy Hot? I was talking myself into a hole.

So my first task was to buy equipment under the intense scrutiny of an Iron Curtain Suze Orman. Denied! We had radically different views on the value of the US dollar. This was a good thing, because she kept me from frivolously wasting money on small items perhaps more expensive than need be. The downside was a complete denial of treats. "Snickers for $1.29? You know what that buys in Romania? Denied!"

I didn't know how much a new bike would cost, but figured

it would surely cost more than the $200 Aurelia allocated for it. I protested, "I need to get something of fair quality. You expect me to ride safely for 1,500 miles on a bike that costs less than shoes you wear to a nightclub?"

"You said 500 miles," she countered.

"It's not just the ride," I pointed out, "it's also training. I'll probably need a grand for everything."

"What?" she squeaked in outrage. "You think I'm made of Benjamins?"

"You paid $500 for a leather coat you've never worn," I protested. "And never will, 'cause this is Las Vegas. Hello? It's hot here."

At least the leather coat made a good blanket for my night on the couch.

There were five bike shops in Las Vegas. We visited them all, with increasingly maddening results. Only two offered a 'cheap' bike for $3000. I refused to believe that bikes cost that much when something like 40% of Las Vegas homes had mortgages underwater. But compared to prices closer to the Strip, these were bargains.

Finally we went to the Schwinn dealer. I grew up with Schwinn bikes and knew they weren't titanium-alloy or whatever Schwarzenegger's Terminator was made of. The show floor was very wide and open, a refreshing change from the crowded boutique-style shops Vegas preferred. After having already wasted hours in fruitless searching, we wasted no more and marched right up to the counter. There waited a man of perhaps sixty, wearing a sweater and sporting a mustache. He looked very professorial.

"Good afternoon," I said. "I would like to see the bikes you have under $1,000."

"Certainly," he said, moving around the counter. We walked down row upon row of bicycles and he pointed out numerous delicate plastic and aluminum pink things with ribbons and stuff for little girls.

"I'm sorry," I clarified. "I meant for me. I'm doing a 500-mile ride."

He laughed. I couldn't believe it. He laughed at a customer!

"People in Vegas sure are dreamers," he said, snuffling back more chuckles, "But really, come on."

This from a sixty-something guy? Didn't he recall a different world than post-building nuthouse Vegas? I began to fear my visions of a perfect vacation by immersing myself into Midwestern wholesomeness as likely as meeting Elvis. OK, bad example.

Finally we found a mom and pop store we liked. The couple was extremely young, but the moniker still fit. Both were dubious of such a 'cheap' bike, but offered to try. Most likely they wanted to get their hooks into fresh meat. Using catalogues the lady helped me select a bike for a 'piddly' $800.

"This will be a good starter bike," she said, or rather grudgingly admitted. "But before the year is out you'll want to upgrade to a real bike."

Her comment was so offhand as to be honest.

"The price includes a custom fit to your gait when it comes in. And we generously give away a free water bottle."

The indicated water bottle was crammed with their logo, address, email address, and QR code.

"Do you need all the gear, too?"

"Yes," I said, grimacing. I was right to cringe because the list of necessaries was extensive. But I got moderately priced equipment in the form of a portable tire repair kit—imperative when biking alone through Nevada's desert wastes—a tire pump, a helmet, a bike rack for the Jeep, and other miscellaneous odds and ends. I also opted for the heavy-duty lock, since we had been robbed eight times in our three years in Vegas.

"Say, can I order a bike seat that's bigger? These are all so small and hard."

"The big ones are soft and squishy for short rides," she explained. "On long rides butts move around too much."

"But I have a little butt," I protested weakly. She looked dubious at this claim. Perhaps worse, Aurelia failed to contain a squeaking laugh.

"It's all about friction, you see," she continued. "Smaller surface area means less friction. You don't want friction down there."

"No, I don't think I do," I agreed. "So a tiny, rock-hard seat guarantees no friction?"

"Oh, no," she scoffed, laughing at the absurdity of the idea. "There's no guarantee of anything. Why else do you think there's so many crotch lubes?"

"Crotch lubes?" Aurelia squawked. "Denied!"

The selection of crotch lubes was indeed impressive, not unlike the hair product aisle of a salon with dozens of tubes, tubs, and jars. I was mesmerized by the half-gallon vat of Butt Butter. I expected a broad selection of such things in this city, of course, but at the Adult Toy Emporium or any other of our 500-plus adult establishments.

Skipping the lubes for the moment, I instead loaded up on energy bars. Most were chocolate or yogurt-covered bars. At that early juncture, I didn't realize just how stupid it was to buy any of them. That would come back to haunt me. Like, four times a week for the next four months.

4

The morning after the arrival and fitting of my new bike, I pulled the Jeep into the garage and quietly unhitched the goods from the rear rack. Everything smelled of fresh rubber and crisp plastic. Aurelia tiptoed through the inside door wearing her robe. She looked tired but courteously pretended to be interested.

"I'm sorry I woke you," I apologized.

"Happy with your new toy?" she asked in a tiny, sleepy voice.

"My new *tool*, woman," I corrected with feigned machismo. "I'm sure it pales in comparison with Aaron's bike, but that's OK. As long as it keeps me up with him."

Aurelia yawned. She worked nights as a roulette dealer on the Strip, so I didn't drain her further by expounding upon my excitement over the bike. I did, however, wax poetic over the reason for it.

"You'd like Aaron, you know," I said, leaning over the bike to engage her. "He and his wife Isabel are world travelers. Can you believe they just flew to Argentina to tour wineries and stay with friends? Yes, they somehow have friends in Argentina, unlike the rest of us mere mortals."

To my surprise, Aurelia groaned.

"What?" I asked, suddenly defensive.

"So they're bottles in the club?"

I just stared at her, waiting for an explanation of how people could be bottles in a club.

"You know, spending crazy money on bottle service just to show off. Who goes to Argentina to tour wineries? Go to California."

"Oh, it's nothing like that," I reassured her, "Aaron's a true traveler."

I launched into my best narrator's voice. "No mere collector of refrigerator magnets, he. Aaron is a man who takes the best of other cultures and integrates them into his life. To be sure, his latest example of cultural fusion was downright shocking. For he is a Portlander through and through, which means not only a love of coffee, but an obsession, a mania! He's a monster. Bereft of caffeine, he's the terror of co-workers and small children. Yet after spending a month in Hungary—yes, he's done that, too—he discovered that simple, strong peasant tea suited his stomach better. So back to America he went, and off of coffee he got. Now he drinks tea. His peers call him un-American, but I say it makes him the ultimate American: we're the Melting Pot, are we not? No, I declare Aaron Owen is no bottle on the shelf!"

Aurelia blinked and wavered, having apparently fallen asleep again during my droning. Rousing, she asked, "You done?"

"Yeah," I mumbled. "Sorry."

"It's bottle in the club," she corrected, stifling a giggle. "But really, you haven't seen him in twenty years. What are you hoping for?"

"That he doesn't wear a kilt," I said. "He's very proud of his English ancestry."

Aurelia giggled and sang, "Everybody in the house, represent!"

"You mean represent Las Vegas?" I said, aghast at the notion. "What, wear sequins and bushy sideburns? No way."

"So he's from England?"

"No, but both sides of his family are. His mother traced her lineage back to like the 1300s or something crazy like that. He did attend some college in Nottingham, though."

"Oh, wait," Aurelia exclaimed. "He's that Indiana Jones friend of yours!"

"That's right," I said. "He did an archeological dig in Israel during college. He's also toured the ruins of Machu Picchu and who knows what else."

"So they're rich."

"I don't think so," I said, frowning in thought. "Well, his parents are loaded. His dad's like some genius radiologist. I was always really impressed with how they handled their money. They refused to spoil their kids with stuff, but spared no expense for expanding their world-views. Aaron was smart enough to take advantage of the opportunities his parents gave him. True, he was lost in college for years trying to figure out what he wanted to do with his life. Too many options, I guess. His emails are more about being a Portlander than his job, so I don't know what he ended up doing. I think it has something to do with urban development."

"You'll find out in July."

"Indeed I will!" I exclaimed, patting the seat of my new bike. I frowned at how distressingly hard it felt.

5

Though very impressed with Aaron's world travels, I actually felt ever so slightly on par with them. Luckily, I had been around, too. When I neared thirty, fate stuck her nose into my life in the form of an exotic foreign woman. I was hopelessly—some would say pathetically—smitten and followed her everywhere. In her case that meant further afield than just her native Romania, but also the Caribbean, Mediterranean, and Baltic. Cruise ships were our vehicle, but not as passengers. Oh no: we worked on them, slaving ten months on, two months off. But those two months were free and clear, allowing travel to a variety of other cultures. It was an exciting life, but an exhausting one. After four years the time came to return to land. The question was where to make our fortune? Vegas, baby!

It was all about Aurelia, of course. She was a quad-lingual roulette dealer who had worked in multiple nations before joining ships, and she was pretty. That was a recipe for success. Within a year she had ascended to the best casino on the Las Vegas Strip. A good thing, too, because as a writer my income amounted to little more than a tax write-off. So Las Vegas was good to us, even if we didn't care for living there. But if there was anything I had learned in my travels, it was that every place was worthy unto itself. To think otherwise was simply ethnocentrism.

Thus, I was quite excited to return to Iowa and explore. Growing up in Cedar Rapids, one of the few relatively large cities in Iowa, I had seen no reason to visit tiny farming communities hours away in the far corners of the state. What starry-eyed teen would? So I did not necessarily know my own state. Now I had a chance to see it slowly, fully. Perhaps only now that I was older and wiser could I truly value the merits of small town USA. It was a shame Aurelia would not join me, but an athlete she most certainly was not, nor a camper.

Ah, but it turned out camping would not be so necessary! Aaron informed me that his father had volunteered to drive our support vehicle. This was more than just some guy driving a van full of tents and extra clothes: Doc was bringing a 42-foot RV!

While Aaron and his travels did not necessarily humble me, his father was another matter. Doc was a staggeringly intelligent and insightful man. Further, he was one of the bravest, yet most pragmatic men I knew. He asked the hard questions of life and the world and was not afraid of the answers he found, nor afraid to voice them. Yet this man was no dusty, boring intellect. Doc was a charming, patient conversationalist with a great sense of humor—and a 42-foot RV!

Doc was a world traveler, too, despite humble beginnings as a minister's son. He joined the Air Force and there became a doctor. Of immensely more importance, he also met his best friend and wife Barbara. After their military career they retired to Cedar Rapids, where Doc reinforced his already impressive medical credentials to become a leading radiologist in Eastern Iowa. They also started a family. Though I didn't even meet Aaron until our high school years, I was all but welcomed into their family as an honorary member. This made me exceedingly proud. Over the years their enthusiasm and support had never wavered.

It was shaping up to be a perfect vacation. A perfect opportunity to catch up with an old friend, with hours of quiet biking through gentle countryside. A perfect place to relax after a hard ride, with real showers instead of car washes and a perfect night's sleep in air-conditioned comfort. A perfect reunion. Perfect everything.

But one simply cannot just show up for a 500-mile ride. Training must come first. And my RAGBRAI training was far, far from perfect.

Chapter 2. Training on Planet Vegas

1

I don't know what normal is, but I know what normal is not. Normal is not Las Vegas. This is fundamental to the city, for who goes there to do what they normally do? Las Vegas exists to zipline naked over gyrating topless dancers throwing money at you. That just doesn't happen in normal life. At least not mine.

Nor is the location of Las Vegas normal. Humans were not meant to live there. Nor did they—until us foolish white folks, that is. The Native Americans of the area, the Southern Paiutes, Hualapai, and others, preferred the nearby rocks of Valley of Fire. Yes, they actually preferred living in a place called *Valley of Fire* to Las Vegas. That fact alone spoke volumes.

But live there I did, and training I needed. Aaron biked daily in Portland, and if our time together was going to be perfect, I needed to keep up with him! I began to obsess over training. First came rides around my neighborhood. It seemed an excellent way to start because I could keep the rides short but worthy, because we lived in mountain foothills with some tough inclines. But I had to do a lot more than just thirty minutes during lunch, or an hour after work. I had to do some pretty big rides. I needed rides over fifty miles, even up to eighty. That meant exiting the city, and that meant hostile terrain.

For my first trip into the wild I selected the Red Rock Canyon Scenic Byway. This was actually right next to the city sprawl—beginning at Red Rock Casino and Spa, of course—so I was not too terribly far from civilization should things go awry. I was excited to see how my new bike handled the untamed undulations of tectonic madness that created the candy-striped Rainbow Escarpment and cherry-red upthrusts of Red Rock Canyon. Lonely country, indeed, but simply gorgeous. The bike worked great for being so 'cheap'. I began hitting that route several times a week, gleefully inching up the mileage each time. A month passed and the heat level rose. It soon became the defining issue of each ride. But I persevered for adventure, for Aaron, for me.

The time came for a big ride. A thirty miler on the Scenic Byway would max out the loop. I was eager to conquer that road. But most of all, I was eager to plumb that greatest biking mystery of all. For, unbeknownst to my dear Aurelia, I had secretly bought some crotch lube. Even more secretly—so secret I didn't dare admit it even to myself—I was excited to try it. I didn't exactly know why chamois cream intrigued me so, but I was eager to find out.

A chamois was simply the name for the cushion built into biking-specific shorts: a big, smooth pad in the crotch. Somehow, somewhere, lubricant was involved. I'd never before devoted time to exploration of this uniquely biking ritual. Though I had worn some pretty outlandish stuff—generally in the privacy of my own bedroom—this was a new one.

Chamois creams had exciting names. Vegas names. Most were anatomically-minded—as if deep down we aren't all anatomically-minded—like Assos, DZ Nuts, or Butt Paste. Others were playfully animalistic, such as Udderly S-MOO-th.

Some combined both, a la Bag Balm. I'm not afraid to admit that Beljum Hard Core Budder intimidated me, as did the description for Friction Freedom: 'helps heal and manage existing saddle sores, while preventing chafing, and bacterial and fungal infections that cause hot spots and infections.' Did I really want to risk all that for Aaron, or any reason whatsoever? In the end I opted for the apparent leader of the pack, Chamois Butt'r. Even then I was scared because it came in little portable containers that looked distressingly like a suppository.

My first dilemma was figuring out if I wore underwear with the bike shorts or not. I decided in true American fashion that more is better, which meant if one layer was safe, two was safer. I wore underwear. Feeling exceedingly self-conscious, I squirted a bunch of Chamois Butt'r down there. Chafing even as I walked around the Jeep did not bode well.

Things immediately took a turn for the worse.

By mile six, I had to stop. This was a common turn around point for day-trippers as it was the location of a beautiful scenic overlook. I didn't stop to enjoy the gaping views of tectonic splendor and wildly diverse color, but rather to adjust my smarting crotch and answer nature.

It was hot outside, of course. Though only March, the sun already burned a good hundred degrees in the Mojave Desert. Heat waves bounced off the hard earth with more intensity than even from the highway's black asphalt. Crazy anything could grow in that dirt. Few things did, actually, and all were ornery as hell. If something grew, it had spikes. If it didn't have spikes, it had hide thick as an elephant's. Supposedly, animals lived out there, burrowing things like lizards, kangaroo rats or jackrabbits. A rather vocal non-profit organization insisted this was the habitat of the endangered desert tortoise, but I didn't believe it. I had been hiking these wastes for years and hadn't seen a thing, including tracks. To this day I maintain that tortoises don't exist.

So, sweating and panting, I eased my aching ass off the bike and unbuckled my helmet. The straps dangled down my cheeks to scratch off the sunblock, but breathing came more easily. I stiffly proceeded to the toilets, keenly aware of suffering some sort of diaper rash. I couldn't remember the last time I had that, but was pretty sure it sucked then, too.

The facilities were merely pit latrines, if immaculately maintained. The concrete structure provided a measure of relief from the heat, but it was still more than hot enough to keep the pit's contents fresher than I cared to smell. I stood before the latrine and looked down to deal with the rather intimidating bike shorts. There was no fly in the chamois, of course, just soggy cloth and spandex stretched perversely across my privates, smashing them into forms no man ever wants to see. True, people probably paid for that in Vegas, but I was not one of them. I tried not to dwell on the fact that I was doing it to myself, for free, for Aaron. I leaned forward to get a better look at my brutalized package.

Mistake.

My helmet tumbled from my head, dropping directly into the latrine. The fall was a clean one, missing the rim entirely to plummet directly into the pit. It landed with a sickening, squishy thump. I blinked in disbelief, staring down at my new $65 helmet perched neatly atop a rising mound of feces. This was not good. This was distinctly bad. And I had twenty-four more miles to go!

Turns out head safety wasn't the problem. The problem was a wild burro attack. Yes, a wild burro attack. I sensed that maybe, just maybe, Aaron's training in Oregon presented less challenges for him. Bigfoot, maybe.

It happened at mile twenty. I had reached the end of the Scenic Byway and already turned back, pausing at a rather enchanting notch between mountains that obviously had a hidden water source somewhere. A few lonely willow trees rose up, but, confused and defeated, drooped back down to the rocky earth and rough scrub. It was the only roadside shade on the entire Scenic Byway, other than the manufactured overlook back at mile six.

Severely stiff and crotch blazing, I eased off my bike. Groaning, I awkwardly squatted to remove a snack from a seat bag on the bike. Progress was even more painfully slow than slogging up miles-long hills against thirty mile per hour winds. Finally I retrieved my treasure and grinned through sun-cracked lips.

The euphoria was short-lived. The energy bar was nothing more than a gooey mess, like a cookie pulled too soon from the oven. Grunting and still squatting like some sort of animal, I licked the hot gunk from the wrapper. I carefully forced out of my mind worries about training rides when summer hit. This was only early spring, after all.

I spied the burro half a mile away through the scrub brush, nuzzling a cholla. He spied me, too, and began noisily honking. The sound carried easily over the dead, scorched earth. He began trotting towards me until perhaps a hundred feet away. Then he charged.

Panic flashed through me. The burro moved incredibly fast. I could never outrun him—certainly not with a funky diaper rash—and I doubted I could start on my bike with anything approaching alacrity. I wasn't sure what to do. I considered briefly sitting down and crying, but sitting would hurt worse than anything the burro would do. So I frantically hobbled to a desert-willow and peeked around the trunk. At least that would break the wild beast's charge.

I never underestimated wild animals in Nevada, for I had been attacked by some pretty benign-seeming beasts. Once a horde of bunnies nearly ended my life. Yes, really. The worst, though, was being attacked by an angry stallion who thought I was chasing his fillies. That had been absolutely terrifying, seeing such a huge, magnificent animal overtly displaying aggressive behavior and me being several miles of cross-country running from my Jeep. I survived that, so there was nothing to worry about in a lousy mule, right?

Wrong.

The charging burro was easily an eight hundred pound wild animal. Many reached a thousand pounds. All were hardened survivors of the worst land nature had to offer. I had seen cute, fuzzy youngsters placidly snacking on cactus thorns the size of my fingers. I didn't want to mess with anything that had a mouth that tough. He could have bitten right through my helmet, if I still had one. I didn't even want to imagine a kick from those hooves.

The burro got about twenty feet away and slowed. Finally

he stopped and eyed me. I eyed him back from behind the relative safety of the tree.

He appeared young because his coat was pretty and trim and he was slender. Most wild burros I'd seen had barrel chests and shaggy coats. His neck had a rough spot, as if something had tried to take him down. It looked exactly like a predator's mark, and it gleamed. Yes, that was blood. For sure it was. I didn't know what could take a chunk out of an animal that big, and I didn't want to find out. There were no big predators in the Mojave, unless you counted the aggregate mass of a coyote pack. That was unlikely, but not impossible.

The burro seemed content to just observe. Then he became vocal. He honked at me. Presumably he associated humans with food. I told him I didn't have anything to eat, which was true. He didn't believe me. Nor would he shut up about it. It's rare to find someone who talks more than me. And in the animal kingdom? You have to look for screaming monkeys and stuff. A long time passed, and he seemed in no hurry to leave. I, on the other hand, thought leaving most prudent.

But, simply put, I couldn't take any more chafing. I just couldn't. Squatting beneath the desert-willow, I stripped off my loathsome chamois. Decency was irrelevant as it was just the burro and me.

If only.

Suddenly, and for the first time in hours, cars appeared on the Scenic Byway. What were the odds they would pass at this one and only moment? But life could be mean like that. The cars whizzed by as my white, über-lubed butt glowed brilliantly from the shade of the tree. But removing my soggy underwear provided instant relief, and that mattered more than anything else. I smashed the squishy underwear into the bike satchel and oh-so-carefully remounted. I delicately rubbed my tender privates atop the bike saddle. Everything slid properly over the lubricated chamois. I sighed. The burro approved with a honk. I was glad he couldn't speak English.

All that was just a single thirty-mile ride! Of course, it got worse. Much, much worse.

2

But I learned. I learned that the proper and generous application of Chamois Butt'r prevented saddle sores. I learned that, as I've always maintained, underwear is just in the way. I also learned that sometimes Mom was right.

Like so many rebellious youths, I had scoffed when Mom told me drinking from the garden hose would cause a bacterial invasion that would devour my flesh and eat my brains. I did it anyway. I'm fine. I also scoffed when Mom told me that not wearing a hat would cause frost bite that would destroy my flesh and freeze my brains. Soon as she wasn't looking, off came the hat. Mom also told me to wear a helmet when riding my bike. Really, Mom. Just how uncool do you want your son to be?

But I learned that helmets were necessary. Very, very necessary.

I was beginning at the Red Rock Canyon Scenic Byway. A traffic light separated the parking lot from the desert road. I neared the traffic signal and slowed on the sidewalk, waiting for a green light. My bike wavered a bit, but my balance was good. My distance calibration needed some work, though. The handlebar met a pole and jerked the front wheel perpendicular to my forward momentum. In a blink I was falling backwards to the pavement. My head smacked onto the sidewalk with a thunderous CRACK!

I lay there a moment, seeing stars. I had never seen stars like that before. It defied credulity that my head hit so brutally hard. Damn you, physics! Whiplash... at three miles per hour! But while my bike was only moving slowly, my body had fallen much faster, with my head whipping down with crushing force. Had I not been wearing a helmet I would have been really and truly damaged. What followed was a rare moment of sobriety. And, of course, yet another trip to the store to buy yet another helmet.

So I learned to give it up to Mom on that one.

I also learned to hate Vegas cyclists.

3

Red Rock Canyon Scenic Byway. Saturday morning. 7 a.m. The parking lot was full. A long line of men and women in brilliant spandex jerseys snaked out of the Starbucks. Small clusters talked to each other, but that rarely meant meaningful conversation. Most merely waited for the other to stop talking so they could brag about their bike and gear.

I generally avoided the Scenic Byway on weekends because it was a favorite cruising destination for Las Vegans and tourists. The road rumbled with speeding Lamborghinis,

Ferraris, and Harleys. Staying alive in all that meant sticking to the shoulder. After half an hour I passed the scenic stop with its helmet-eating latrine. The area was brimming with bicyclists already turning back. Go on, little riders, shell out $3000 worth of bike, and another $1,000 worth of clothing, just to stop and turn around for only an hour ride. Go on, I say! These bikers were all show and no substance. I had faced a wild burro and survived! Go ahead, little people, discuss your expensive doodads at Starbucks. I'm busy being awesome.

Enter: rude awakening.

A block of riders overtook me, dominating the shoulder by riding double-wide, handlebar to handlebar. A single cyclist rode at the fore, like Death himself on a pale bike, leading the Riders of the Apocalypse. They numbered not four, but eleven: leader crying havoc before ten instruments of Armageddon, crushing and casting aside all in their path.

Exit: stage right.

Forced off the shoulder at top speed, I was nearly hurled into a rugged washout twenty feet deep. By sheer luck—and adrenaline—I managed to collapse instead of fly. Pain blasted through me as I hit the crumbling bank of rocks, sliding right up to the very edge. I felt each and every rock, but it was better than a similar crunch after a twenty-foot fall. The hell riders zoomed past my head, a blur of snapping yellow jerseys and disdain, their cadence booming into the desert, crossing the wastes and echoing off distant mountains.

"Who's Lance?"
"WE'RE LANCE!"

"Who's Lance?"
"WE'RE LANCE!"
"How many?"
"SEVEN!"
"How many?"
"SEVEN!"

Surely this wasn't what I was going to encounter on RAGBRAI: herds of Lance Armstrong wanna-bes? Only then did it occur to me I would be one of a minimum of 10,000 simultaneous riders. My vision blurred, only to refocus on recollections of one Tour de France rider falling and dozens of poor, following riders tumbling into him. I wasn't prepared for that at all!

4

But when things don't go your way in Vegas, nobody calls it quits. We double down. In my case, I swapped the Scenic Byway's thirty miles of all but lonely desert for the unlimited milage of freakin' aliens-only desert. Literally. I chose the wastes north of Las Vegas, mere miles from Area 51 and its supposed UFO sightings. This was a place so God-forsaken that the U.S. military continued to test top-secret stuff out there, knowing no normal human would ever dare go there. So for Aaron I risked getting abducted by aliens. Fortunately, no anal probes occurred. At that point my butt was so numb I probably wouldn't have noticed anyway. But something particularly loathsome did occur.

It was on my longest training ride, an eighty-five miler. I started the ride at 3:40 a.m. That didn't mean I woke up at 3:40, oh no. It was an hour drive just to get to my starting point. So up at 2:30 I was, knowing how bad the heat would get. Or I thought I did. You never really prepare yourself for heat pushing 130°, you just think you do.

I parked the Jeep on the side of the road at mile marker 1. It was still dark. Stars were visible to the north and west, but already fading into the rosy glow of the east. To the south lay Las Vegas, source of enough light to make the cosmos squint. This place was so awful that after 119 nuclear blasts the landscape hadn't noticeably changed. So they set off 500 more underground.

By flashlight I readied my hydration backpack with a forty-ounce bladder. Two ice packs were tucked within to keep it all relatively cool, for after a few hours in that heat water could brew tea. I brought some gel-like globules called Gu-Chomps, hoping to swallow the scalding hot mass they would inevitably become. For lunch I had a Pemmican-brand energy bar. This was carefully devoid of chocolate or yogurt or anything else that would melt. Thus my reward at halfway—43 miles!—was basically a sack of oats, fat, and sugar compressed into a bar. For you, Aaron.

I sprayed myself liberally with half a can of 50 SPF sunblock—an odd thing to do in the blackness of night—wet my lips with 50 SPF Chapstick, and was ready to go. Out there nature provided no shade whatsoever. Well, that wasn't entirely true. At mile fifty-something—beyond the turn-around point— was a stagnant oasis of crusty water laden with violent amoebas.

There rose three sorry-looking trees and five signs warning the water was toxic.

Though starting in darkness, I wasn't worried about being struck by a car. My bike had been haphazardly painted Day-Glo green and would easily catch headlights. Who would drive out there at this hour anyway? At any hour? Only a single DNR truck forced to do so. I considered the solitude. The quiet of the desert was awesome, humbling, frightening. This was a rare place where man held no sway, but only left evidence of passage to elsewhere. Yet the silence was deeper than merely the absence of man. It was the rarified silence of no life at all. No plants to rustle, no crickets to chirp, no birds to cry. The ribbon of asphalt undulated alone across bone-dry washes and through barren mountains of exposed rock upthrust to reveal literally four billion years of past life. *Past* life.

Such a profound record of life's fecundity surrounded me. Where had it all gone? Why?

The answer rose presently. Sunlight crawled over the 'cool' 85° landscape with destroying heat, stirred brutally hot winds and lethal aridity. Out there people had been found dead with water still in their possession. The severe dryness sucked all moisture from their bodies faster than drinking could replenish it.

Another hour or so the thermometer registered 115°. Heat rebounding off the dead earth added uncharted degrees. Surprising, then, was encountering the first sight of life. Buzzards circled up ahead. No, not buzzards, but ravens: huge, black, and bigger than my fourteen-pound cats. I rode towards them, wondering for what they were waiting to die. But do not ask for whom the bell tolls: it tolls for thee. At mile marker 33 I passed a dead jackrabbit the size of a beagle. The poor creature was smashed, innards steaming in the sun. It freaked me out.

Just two hours later it would freak me out far, far more. But more on that later.

5

Over the course of four months of nearly constant riding, I discovered that I hated biking. It wasn't just the Vegas riders, though that was a big part of it. It wasn't even the heat, though that was an even bigger part of it. No, I loathed biking because my rides had almost universally been in winds ranging from twenty to thirty miles per hour—on a good day. Nothing broke the wind for hundreds of miles in all directions of Vegas, so gusts fanned out over the wastes to push you off the road and belittle your puniness of size and effort. When mountains interfered they made it worse, channeling the winds into tunnels that roared through the barren passes I labored through. Biking was not fun. It was torture.

But all that was done. The time had come to pack away the hateful skin-searing crotch-killer. Dismembering the bike was a surprisingly satisfying experience. My victory was ultimately denied, however. The last pedal refused to come off. I struggled so mightily that I broke the ratchet! After a trip to the store and much profanity I resumed my effort, only to be continually defeated. Finally I just shoved the frame into the slender box, scraping the pedal down the side. It burst through the cardboard. With devilish glee I drew a band-aid over the area and added a cartoon-style bubble caption shouting "$@&%!"

But the drama wasn't done. The shipping company failed to arrive and pick up the wounded box. Because timing was critical in this step, I called them in a panic.

"You didn't pick up my parcel!" I cried into the phone. "It's gotta be shipped by today or it won't make it on time."

"Our apologies," replied a nasally man through the phone. "What is the address?"

"Shiny Skies Drive," I replied hastily.

"Chinese Guys Drive," the voice repeated. "Yes, my notes say they went there yesterday and found no package."

"Shiny Skies," I repeated with emphasis.

"Chinese Guys."

"Skies, man!" I burst out. "Isn't this Las Vegas? Clear skies, as in no clouds. The sun shines here all the damn time. Shiny skies."

"Of course, sir. Our apologies. We will send a truck to pick up your parcel at Chinese Guys Drive, in sunny Las Vegas. Thank you for your business."

Irrationally angry, I shoved the box into the Jeep and hauled it straight to the transport company's office. I was thrilled to get rid of the thing. I never wanted to see it again. But boy, would I. A week's worth of loathsome riding awaited.

Aaron better be worth it.

But rid of the toil of actual riding, and with the assistance of much rum, happy dreams of biking bubbled to the surface. I grew enthusiastic anew and began scouring the internet for bits and pieces of trivia or advice. Eventually I clicked on the official map of elevation. My jaw dropped.

RAGBRAI claimed that Day 1 had 4,298 feet of elevation gain over 59.5 miles. According to the source I had been training with, MapMyRIDE.com, the route only climbed 1,400 feet. RAGBRAI was going to be 66% harder than I thought. In fact, Day 1 and Day 2 were both harder than any single day of Colorado's famed Ride the Rockies! Though the latter crested several mountain passes, its total elevation gain only beat RAGBRAI by 400 measly feet.

I tried to calm myself. I knew this. I was raised in Iowa. Everyone not from Iowa stereotyped it as flat as a pancake. Such riders faced one hell of a learning curve! There are easily eighty rivers in Iowa, with each and every one carving its own valley—a valley to pedal out of. Then, of course, there were the two monsters bordering the state: the Muddy Missouri and the Mighty Mississippi. 10,000 years ago the glaciers receded and let those bad boys loose. Since then they've wreaked havoc unchecked, carving and moving and carving again. And carving power did they have: the Mississippi alone tapped a whopping thirty-two American states and two Canadian provinces to make the fourth greatest drainage on the planet.

None of it mattered. It was too late to chicken out. I wondered what else I would encounter that I hadn't counted on. As a travel writer, I was used to things not going as expected. After exploring fifty-some nations, I never would have dreamed that Iowa would hold some of my greatest surprises!

6

Saturday, July 23rd. Glenwood, Iowa. Such was the date and place, one day prior to the celebrated tire dip. The Midwest's largest bike expo—take that, Chicago—was set up in the parking lot of the Glenwood Community High School. After goodbye hugs from my shuttling parents—and Mom's last minute check that I had a helmet—I said goodbye, shouldered my week's worth of gear, and strode down to the sprawling series of tents, canopies, and kiosks.

Aaron had texted me to meet him at the bike delivery area. For some reason cell phone reception was spotty in Glenwood, but the message squeaked through. Finding the appropriate tents among the many presented no challenge, as the dozens of slender boxes stacked fifty yards deep demanded attention. Perfectly easy.

I worked my way through the milling crowd towards the bike delivery. Hundreds of people had already arrived despite the early hour and the rain. The clouds above were thick and twisted, like a giant nebulous towel being wrung over yonder. Fortunately, above us directly it was only drizzling. It was delightful to this desert rat. Perfectly refreshing.

A surprisingly small tent was allocated for the organizing and distribution of all the shipped bikes. Several enthusiastic men and women waited with clipboards, ready to check off names and send the eager young men into the piles of boxes to muscle out specific parcels. Not seeing Aaron anywhere nearby, I went ahead with the process. Because the expo had only officially opened thirty minutes ago, there was no wait. Perfect!

Yes, it was all going as planned. After months of slaving and sweating, planning and stressing, it was all going to be as perfect as I had imagined.

A stranger approached. He was of average height but much bigger build. His huge shoulders and arms said bodybuilder, but his equally huge belly admitted those were days past. The man's dress and manner were rather slovenly, his face unshaven. All his hair was shot with grey, be it on his head, on his face, or protruding from his nose. A spandex biking jersey strained ludicrously over his paunch, the pattern of Vincent Van Gogh's Starry Night stretching stars into large, furry comets around a moon bloated to a white super giant. He seemed oddly intent on me.

He moved through the crowd, snarfing down a cheap microwave burrito. Under one armpit was the smashed wrapper of another. He finally made eye contact with me. His gaze was bold and handsome, intense beneath a strong brow. He quickly crammed the remains of the meal into his mouth—meaning the entire second half of the burrito—swallowing it in a painfully forced gulp. The stranger beamed at me and offered his hand. His vice-like grip made me squirm.

"I'm Cheek!" he said enthusiastically. "I'll be riding with you!"

Who the hell was this?

Books by Brian David Bruns

Fiction:
The Gothic Shift
In the House of Leviathan
The Widow of Half Hill

Nonfiction:
Cruise Confidential
Ship for Brains
Unsinkable Mister Brown
High Seas Drifter
Cruise a la Carte

Comstock Phantoms:
True Ghost Stories of Virginia City, NV

Rumble Yell:
Discovering America's Biggest Bike Ride

Praise for Brian David Bruns

"This man has seen it all."
- *ABC 20/20*

"*Cruise Confidential* is a very funny, behind-the-scenes exploration of a cruise ship."
- *Booklist*

"Bruns has the science of tension building down to an art form. I was squirming in my seat to find out what would happen in the end."
- *Reader's Favorite Reviews*

"An absorbing story that sacrifices light predictability for depth and solid development.
- *Midwest Book Reviews*

"I couldn't put it down."
- *Chicago Sun-Times*

"A delightful balance of whimsy and the grotesque, with a glimmer of moonstruck romance. Bruns creates well-imagined, realistic settings for his lively characters."
- *Kirkus Reviews*

Copyright

Library of Congress Cataloguing-in-Publication Data
    Bruns, Brian David
    2nd ed.
    Produced by World Waters

ISBN (print edition): 9781522073871
ISBN (ebook): 9781311570192

    1. Travel/Essay 2. Cruise Ships—Humor

Printed in Great Britain
by Amazon